MW01255062

Orchestrating Connection

Praise for Orchestrating Connection

"No one could write a book titled *Orchestrating Connection* better than David Homan, whom I have described as the 'connector in chief.' David is truly the ultimate architect and implementer of a system to help build purposeful communities. We can all learn from what he describes in this wonderful, compelling, and inspirational book."

GENERAL DAVID PETRAEUS, US Army (Ret.), former commander of Multi-National Force – Iraq and International Security Assistance Force and U.S. Forces – Afghanistan, former director of the Central Intelligence Agency, coauthor of *Conflict: The Evolution of Warfare from 1945 to Gaza*

"In team sports, you may excel as an individual, but you only win as a tight-knit group. That group, in essence, is a community because what you bring to the game and how you act off the court all informs that subtle dynamic of what makes a group champions. *Orchestrating Connection* systematically creates the rituals for self-work to develop self-worth, and for how we master our network to create teams that champion us as we champion them."

CANDACE PARKER, former WNBA forward, two-time Olympic gold medalist, sports anchor, author of *The Can-Do Mindset*

"This book is essential reading for everyone on this journey of life, and especially those feeling restless in big or seemingly quiet ways, seeking to live a more connected life—to community and to purpose. It is instructional without being didactic—and is inspirational, thanks to how much you share fully personal experiences. Thank you on behalf of a generation, or more, for writing a playbook for us all."

RACHEL GERROL, CEO and co-founder of NEXUS

"Wow. I haven't been this inspired about the future of human connection since I read *The Art of Gathering* by Priya Parker. The prose shifts easily between gripping stories and practical insights on human connection. Required reading for anyone who loves bringing people together."

ANDY DUNN, founding CEO of Pie and Bonobos, author of *Burn Rate: Launching a Startup and Losing My Mind*

"My life has been about family, bringing children joy and strengthening communities, both as a business leader and philanthropist. Our world needs new perspectives on how to bring passionate, driven leaders together, and this book delivers them. The work one must do personally, and with whom one surrounds oneself, is crucial to create ethical, accountable standards for the evolution of our society. *Orchestrating Connection* takes what we know and puts it together in a way that can bring about a systemic change in perspective."

ALAN HASSENFELD, former chairman and CEO of Hasbro

"Leadership in philanthropy is fundamentally about gathering and empowering others to help. This is what *Orchestrating Connection* is about: the crucial insight that surrounding yourself with the 'right' people starts with you and resonates outward based on integrity and your principles, like the concentric rings around a pebble thrown into a pond. David Homan's work on the board of the Arthur Miller Foundation has given us invaluable insights into how giving can be contagious, given the right strategies. I endorse the benefits of this book's guidance because I have seen them in action."

REBECCA MILLER, filmmaker, activist, and philanthropist

"As loneliness levels are rising, exacting a high price from individuals and society, *Orchestrating Connection* provides the antidote we need. Rigorous, engaging, essential!"

TAL BEN-SHAHAR, author *Happier* and *Being Happy*, teacher, and founder of the Happiness Studies Academy

"We've said it from day one at Rent the Runway: 'we're not just a closet; we're a community.' Even though we have millions of members, that community feels tightly knit, because we have crafted it around our purpose—to not just disrupt the fashion industry but to empower women—and a spirit of generosity, inspiration, and support. The practical steps and guidance offered in *Orchestrating Connection* match so closely to how we've gone about building RTR. I wish we'd had a playbook like this! Highly recommended for any founder looking to make a dent in their industry or the world by purposefully and thoughtfully bringing their customers together."

JENNIFER HYMAN, co-founder and CEO of Rent the Runway

ORCHESTRATING
CONNECTION

How to Build
PURPOSEFUL COMMUNITY
in a Tribal World

DAVID HOMAN & NOAH ASKIN

NEW YORK

LONDON • NASHVILLE • MELBOURNE • VANCOUVER

ORCHESTRATING CONNECTION

How to Build PURPOSEFUL COMMUNITY in a Tribal World

© 2025 David Homan and Noah Askin

All rights reserved. No part of this book may be used or reproduced in any manner whatsoever without prior written permission from the authors or publisher, except in the case of brief quotations in critical articles and reviews.

Without in any way limiting the authors' exclusive rights under copyright, any use of this publication to "train" generative artificial intelligence (AI) technologies to generate text is expressly prohibited. The authors reserve all rights to license uses of this work for generative AI training and development of machine learning language models.

Published in New York City, New York, by Morgan James Publishing. Morgan James is a trademark of Morgan James, LLC. www.MorganJamesPublishing.com

Proudly distributed by Publishers Group West®

A FREE ebook edition is available for you or a friend with the purchase of this print book.

CLEARLY SIGN YOUR NAME ABOVE

Instructions to claim your free ebook edition:
1. Visit MorganJamesBOGO.com
2. Sign your name CLEARLY in the space above
3. Complete the form and submit a photo of this entire page
4. You or your friend can download the ebook to your preferred device

ISBN-13: 978-1-636-98681-4 (paperback)
ISBN-13: 978-1-636-98682-1 (ebook)
Library of Congress Control Number
(LCCN): 2025933845
LC record available at https://lccn.loc.
gov/2025933845

Cover Design by:
Jason Simon

Interior Design by:
Chris Treccani
www.3dogcreative.net

Morgan James is a proud partner of Habitat for Humanity Peninsula and Greater Williamsburg. Partners in building since 2006.

Get involved today! Visit: www.morgan-james-publishing.com/giving-back

To those who felt they had a superpower no one else saw, but kept silent. We see you. This book is dedicated to every person who gave more than they asked in return. To each individual who set in motion ripples upon ripples that changed the world, while others took the credit. And most especially, to everyone who believed in our "community of communities" and gave their energy and time in the growth of Orchestrated Connecting.

—D. H.

For Heidi, Micah, and Max

—N. A.

Attention is the rarest and purest form of generosity.

—SIMONE WEIL

Contents

Preface

A nightmare...
You walk out onto a concert stage, dressed immaculately. A Steinway grand piano awaits, lid open, gleaming under the stage lights. The barely lit audience, obscured by the lights, erupts in applause. A standing ovation even before you begin. It feels like it lasts minutes. You sit, hands trembling above the keys, as the silence closes in and expectation builds. You smile gently, trying to breathe and calm your nerves.

The problem: you can't play piano. Not really. The instrument, an old acquaintance from your youth, is now entirely unfamiliar. Plus, "Für Elise," should you be able to pluck it from the depths of your memory, isn't exactly concert hall material.

You begin to feel a gnawing hollowness; the crowd, now faceless in the dark, is made up entirely of strangers. What should be your moment of glory is instead a chilling realization of your solitude.

You wake.

🎼 🎼 🎼

In our experience, success rarely comes from moments of isolated brilliance. Instead, it's the product of countless encounters, small acts of trust, calculated risks, and critical introductions that align to support you when the stakes are highest. For every dreamer with their sights set on the grand stage—be it Carnegie Hall, the

Royal Albert Hall, or one of life's smaller venues—true mastery emerges only when you've perfected your instrument *and* you're ready to share the journey, supported by those around you. It's these connections and purposeful bonds that prepare you for the pivotal moments.

You begin by doing whatever is necessary to be ready to take that risk and put yourself in the spotlight. Ready for criticism. Ready for feedback. Ready to pick yourself up over and over again, practicing and perfecting until you find just the right way to play the notes.

To make your life a symphony, though, you need more than technical precision. You need to move from perfecting your own instrument to being able to see the larger perspectives necessary to succeed. You need to learn to harmonize, to listen intently, and to feel the pulse of a collective. To resonate with others. Your instrument will become a voice among voices, each adding depth and nuance to a shared vision.

Being a *part* of a community is like being that musician, perfecting your own instrument while collaborating and coordinating with those around you. *Building* purposeful community is akin to conducting an orchestra: you understand each player's strengths, draw out their best, and ensure all are aligned with the larger composition. A conductor, like a true community builder, knows the importance of balance—when to step forward, when to step back, and how to inspire cohesion amid individual differences. Grounding the orchestra and seeing the flow from section to section, the conductor plays nothing yet represents everything.

Much like a single melody is enriched by an entire orchestra, when you thoughtfully surround yourself with others who share, enhance, or even challenge your vision and your purpose, you amplify their reach, as well as your own. Finding and achieving genuine purpose is therefore about cultivating meaningful connections that resonate with your values and ambitions.

Of course, you aren't likely to start by trying to write a symphony. It would be too overwhelming. However, if you begin with your own instrument, your own melody, and build, you can eventually find your way to your symphony. You integrate your melody into each part of your orchestra and, ideally, grow from there.

To build a symphony, there is an assumption that each player can play their part perfectly and be able to hear not only themselves and everyone in their section but also the rest of the orchestra playing in balance with them. Hearing more than just your own part is a special skill, incredibly hard to achieve even for the best of musicians, as you don't practice in a group when you're a kid; you practice alone.

Because of this, and because of its complexity, the thought of conducting is often terrifying, even to master musicians. Yet, once you can gain perspective on how the various players and instruments fit together, it becomes more approachable. And, when it comes to your relationships and ultimately your community, as you gain perspective on how these connections work in your life and each other's lives, you can start to orchestrate them more effectively. Just like orchestra sections.

Orchestration at the Core

Intentional community-building is the art of crafting a symphony from life's cacophony. You don't need to found a company, create a masterpiece, make millions, or qualify for the Olympics to make your life purposeful. Instead, focus on discovering your melody, honing it, and finding resonance with those who amplify it. By thoughtfully curating and orchestrating your relationships, and communicating why those people have value, you transform from a lone player into the conductor of a shared vision—a symphony not of sound but of purpose, connection, and lasting impact.

So embrace the natural harmony of connectedness and embrace new perspectives on how the various parts, with the right techniques, fit together. Practice your instrument, pay attention to those of others, and see the beauty and music that can be made.

That's how you lead your life as a symphony.

Introduction

Connective Notes

The highest form that civilization can reach is a
seamless web of deserved trust.

—CHARLIE MUNGER

On an otherwise unremarkable Saturday in 2018, David
(co-author of this book) was leading a workshop on building
relationship value as an entrepreneur. The session was for a
group of fifty or so members of a community of start-ups and
industry experts intent on transforming businesses and communities alike. During a conversation about the importance of building
and curating community, a touching story emerged from one of
the mentors in the room, who also happened to be a member of
David's Orchestrated Connecting (OC) community.

The narrative began with a father, stricken with cancer, navigating the uncertainties of a rare diagnosis. Initial prognosis indi-
cated a bleak future, offering an extremely limited timeline for
what remained of his life. Yet, within weeks, this initial outlook
would take a dramatic turn. Thanks to a series of introductions
made by another OC community member—the result of an

impassioned ask made by the individual whose father had can-cer—a cascading network of esteemed medical professionals from multiple countries was activated. They collectively re-evaluated the diagnosis and proposed an optimized care plan, addressing not only the extension of this man's life but also concerns of pain management and well-being.

When probed about their generous act, every individual in this chain of "givers" sidestepped accolades. This hadn't been about granting exclusive access to someone because of their con-nections or status. No one cared about receiving credit, just about providing help.

While the father did not ultimately survive, passing a little less than two years from the initial community activation around his care, his family was able to lay him to rest knowing they did everything they could to help him and improve his chances of a peaceful passing. To this day, the family remembers the enthusias-tic compassion and care given in their time of need, with no asks in return. One of the people who helped and was there for the end of the journey still checks in regularly on the family's Yahrzeit, the Jewish practice of remembering close friends and relatives on the anniversary of their death. His checking-in is a big deal because he doesn't make it one.

Our "Why": Human Connection

Imagine a world where we, like the givers in the story above, all "leaned in" to help, motivated not by what we might receive but by the simple act of giving *as part of a greater purpose*. Perhaps an entire world seems too grandiose or unrealistic? Then instead imagine a community where this is the case, where the culture and how it is perpetuated creates belonging and virtuous cycles of giving. The essence of true generosity lies in its freedom from expectations.

And that, in its purest form, is the foundational "why" behind our mission: to create and cultivate communities bound by purpose and fortified with trusted meaningful relationships. No one is worried about repayment, either in kind or in plaudits. Giving is for the greater good, not for individual gain.

We know that connection amplifies human functioning; individual drive is not nearly as powerful as collective capability. Likewise, a note may be only a single sound, but, when notes connect harmoniously, it's music. And, while Western music consists of twelve notes repeated over and over again, somehow new melodies, harmonies, and incredible songs continuously emerge and define the sound of each generation. We know that music hits at our core, combining our emotions and thoughts and putting us into a unique state when we truly listen—and when we sit in the silence that follows, too. A similar resonance—bringing people together in a shared experience that hits our core—is at the heart of Orchestrated Connecting, the community on which many of the methods and principles shared in this book are based. Each connection adds to that resonance.

Yet, the idea of "connecting" often gets lost in a forest of digital intermediaries or dismissed via association with the more stigmatized "networking." The latter's stigma is hard to shake, despite the fact that the dude "working the room," barely introducing himself while handing out business cards, is surely from a bygone era. Maybe these days he's just sending generic LinkedIn connection requests and superficially relevant, AI-generated, cookie-cutter messages. In any case, we encourage you to put aside your feelings about networking because that's not what we're here to discuss.

"Connection"—specifically, human connection—is a particularly relevant topic as we write. A multi-year pandemic limited our regular human contact to a very small group of carefully chosen others. Our interactions with random strangers—a more common and more important occurrence than many of us realize—were reduced to nearly zero. In the COVID-19 pandemic aftermath, we are less connected and lonelier than at any time in recent history.

Dr. Jeremy Nobel, Harvard Medical School professor and author of *Project UnLonely*, speaks passionately about the importance of community and connection, not for building new bonds but for reducing the immense tragedy that comes from loneliness. When asked about the importance of purpose in building community, Nobel suggests that it is essential for us to better understand not just how we are craving human connection, but also how we are actually want interactions that create and release the kinds of genuine emotions that promote positive well-being, as well as social and emotional growth. To engage our social–emotional well-being, we have to both give and receive empathy; to feel that our words are heard. When this happens, we realize the person with whom we are talking isn't the "other" but someone with whom we can bond.

The benefits of connection and connecting go well beyond individuals, too. In his tome *Sapiens,* Yuval Harari goes so far as to suggest that the formation of collective groups and a connective, shared cultural understanding of the world is how humans have survived to this day. Nothing we do, individually or collectively, can truly function without relationships.

All too often of late, it feels that we have forgotten this, not realizing the consequences of social isolation. Judging by the Surgeon General's alert about a crisis of loneliness in the United States, clearly, we are not having the kinds of interactions that Dr. Nobel is referencing.

It is perhaps unsurprising, then, that there has been a well-documented, decades-long downward trend in the kind of communal spirit that enables these meaningful social interactions. In *Bowling Alone*, Robert Putnam chronicled the substantial drop in Americans' community engagement during the second half of the twentieth century—a trend that has continued through at least the first decades of the twenty-first century. Whether civic or organizational involvement, religious attendance, philanthropic giving, union membership, or even informal social interaction, Putnam demonstrated that Americans were simply participating less and less in community of all kinds.

So, our loneliness challenges were already on the rise before the recent skyrocketing of the capabilities and ubiquity of generative artificial intelligence. This technology will surely play a critical role in our personal and professional lives, further reducing the "need" for what will likely be deemed superfluous interpersonal interaction. But we remain social animals: we seek connection, we hold onto relationships, and we suffer in their absence. *Connection* is a powerful and evocative concept. More powerful still is what connection can do at scale: unlocking that is also part of our "why."

Who Is This Book For?

While we would love anyone and everyone to find something in this book—and we suspect many will—our aim is to address the incorrect assumptions often made about communities, relationships, and the value of aggregating human connection. We do so with a set of practices and principles that you can apply across a wide range of social and communal circumstances.

But let's first start with who this book is *not* for. This book is not for individuals who seek to connect exclusively for personal gain. We believe strongly in the greater good and the importance of every connection being valued. While David's network puts him one degree away from Kevin Bacon, Steven Spielberg, Daniel Day-Lewis, and many other famous and not-so-famous people, he's never asked for an autograph or a special favor from those he's met. Instead, he's asked what he can do to help them achieve or actualize their purpose. No matter how famous or how "normal" you might label the individuals in David's world, the critical idea is that each is valued, not held like some kind of prize. In the end, a deep conversation about a shared value or common cause is far more meaningful than a selfie to share with friends.

To be blunt, what David has sought to do with his approach to community-building in both a simple and sophisticated way is to expound upon a rule most people hope to have: a no-asshole policy. If that resonates with you and your approach to your relationships, this book is for you.

Fundamentally, we want to underscore the importance of being purposeful in your network, redefining it as an ecosystem or a series of overlapping communities. This kind of framing (or reframing) benefits the parents who build friendships taking their kids from Little League to the local pizza parlor. It benefits the friendly neighbor who starts a book club, not because she cares all that much about the books but because she loves the company. It benefits the individual struggling with addiction who would gain a great deal from building stronger bonds that bolster their resolve to heal their illness. It benefits veterans who work to find their place back in society after serving their country. It benefits PTA leaders and alumni network chairpersons. And it benefits the guy starting an over-40 men's group and the recent college graduate who doesn't know anyone in the city she just moved to.

Those are the people this book is for. But they're not the only ones.

Think about your favorite podcast. Maybe you have a few and chances are, if they're on roughly similar topics, you've noticed that the hosts will reference each other and frequently appear on each other's podcasts. That, too, is a community. Noah (our other co-author) listens regularly to the *Huberman Lab* podcast, and the host Andrew Huberman regularly speaks with or about work done by Peter Attia, Rick Rubin, Lex Fridman, Andy Galpin, and many others. Andrew also regularly appears on their podcasts. They have created a community around a shared interest in physical, psychological, neurological, and emotional well-being. Many similar podcaster communities exist.

Podcasts aren't your thing? Think about your local music scene. In Los Angeles, there's an amazing music and comedy venue called Largo. It started in a small, dark, and dingy venue that held maybe one hundred people. But the founder, Mark Flanagan, made the venue an experience for local musicians and comedians, where they could come hang out, perform every once in a while, and contribute to an artistic community. An article about Largo and its founder, written shortly after it moved into a larger theater, noted:

> "In Los Angeles, being a Largo person is much like being a Mac person—those who experience it can't help but buy into its philosophy and talk about it to everyone they know ... Largo artists often refer to the venue as a family environment, and it's an apt description—from Guillermo, who has been sweeping the floors of Largo since its inception, to artists such as Jon Brion and Sarah Silverman, who love the place so much that their residencies can be measured in terms of years rather than weeks."

The artists, performers, and regulars who frequent Largo are absolutely a community.

This book is also for the aspiring founders, podcast hosts, and scene creators. It is for the people who run conferences, host dinner parties, raise money through charity walks/runs, bring people on gallery tours, and do anything and everything that brings people together around a shared vision, value, cause, or purpose.

Community and connection—when done purposefully—represent the acceleration of our value systems aligning. They don't arise simply from a shared location, a responsibility from religious ritual or obligation, or a collection of people you find yourself "stuck" around. In each of those circumstances, which we all regularly find ourselves in, not everyone has a shared purpose or vision. We used to believe community was where we live, where we pray, or what we join because our kids go to the same school. Now, community has the potential to be deeper, based on value systems, on genuine connection, and on the elevation of the whole.

To find value in this book, we are adamant that embracing our methodology is to accept where you are and the work you have done while genuinely questioning whether you are ready to do more work. That work, to be clear, is toward being *more purposeful and intentional in who you are, what you ask for, and who you surround yourself with*, as well as learning how to genuinely ask for what you need.

These are our primary intentions, and we explore them by examining the "soft skills" necessary to "orchestrate" your connections. Many are explained or described through examples of our colleagues and, here and there, our idols. But most of the individuals whose stories we've chosen to share in this book, while extraordinary, are not globally recognized names. They have, however, defined connection, relationship value, and purpose for themselves and for others, and they have regularly changed the way others around them view themselves. We have chosen these individuals because anyone who knows them will surely tell you that their actions, and the impact of those actions, reverberate widely. The effects and the breadth of those reverberations come from their deep understanding of how to build "purposeful community," which we define as any group that creates a sense of belonging with intention.

What we aim to explain is a system—one where the tenets are known and already well practiced in isolation. However, it isn't necessarily easy to put all those principles into practice together. We mean "together" in two ways. First, it's about implementing the tenets at the same time, creating a self-reinforcing system that makes a community thrive. And, second, it's about a collective effort.

This book is not a manual for one person to learn how to network better or run some club or community for personal benefit, even if those benefits are likely to come to those who do. We want to convince you to see your world—your community—as an ecosystem of relationships that you can nurture, define, and activate in order to support you more fully. And one that allows you to simultaneously better support the members of that community, as well.

How to Build Relationships at the Speed of Trust

This book provides a practical, approachable, research-informed blueprint to building, maintaining, and capitalizing on connection at scale. You need not lead your own community, nor be a part of a formal one like those we reference throughout the book. Taking the ideas and applying them to your own social and professional circles is equally as powerful.

Tapping into the basic human desire for connection, David has built a framework for quickly generating trust and gaining alignment across groups of people, all in service of creating a purpose-driven and generous community. Noah uses a modified version of the framework in nearly every class he teaches, as it quickly creates powerful connections and engagement. In the chapters that follow, in addition to learning about a tried-and-true framework for building community, you will read a variety of stories. They all share similar themes of finding the right connections, creating the right conditions, and understanding the immense potential created by the intersection of those two actions. Crucially, the protagonists in the stories all started their community-building journeys with a deep understanding of their own purpose and motivation.

We call the framework and the concept "Orchestrated Connecting." Why "orchestrated"? Because of the word's dual meaning. First, there is a musical quality to the flow of conversation and to relationships more generally. This connotation is intentional: David is trained as a composer and has a master's degree in music, and Noah conducts academic research on creativity in and around music. Second, "orchestrated" implies intentional design and arrangement. Note that it is very much *not* "manipulated" connecting.

The structure of the OC community is useful to analyze as part of this book, but the overarching methodology of why and how it works is what ultimately matters most when it comes to improving your own community, whether formal or informal. Purpose-driven communities—within organizations, across people who share similar visions for the world, or simply among those looking for deeper, more meaningful connection—are increasingly more common, perhaps as a reaction to the increased loneliness felt in recent years. We therefore felt compelled to offer our approach and our understanding of community now, and we intend this book to be useful to everyone from community leaders to individuals simply seeking to develop their personal relationships in a more systematic fashion.

What continues to surprise us is that whatever inspired you to pick up this book has also resonated with some of the most successful, influential connectors on the planet. If they, who ostensibly have little need for assistance in finding community or building their connecting capabilities, feel strongly that the approach we lay out here was not only able to hone their skills but indeed change their own perspective on relationship value, then we can hope this approach will do the same for you.

In the next chapter, the beginning of Part I, you will get a peek at an Orchestrated Connecting event in action. Then, we dive into an overview of how this type of event is made possible— the Orchestrated Connecting blueprint.

We then dig into the importance of finding your purpose, as well as our definition of community.

In Part II, we discuss the principles that lead to maximizing relationship value and how you can implement these principles in your life. Fundamental to these principles is an understanding of community culture and knowing that a thriving culture entails some degree of risk. The Orchestrated Connecting principles include diversity, vulnerability, curiosity, generosity, and gratitude. We illustrate how we have created a culture around these principles, and how ethics guide this framework.

We finish, in Part III, by exploring how Orchestrated Connecting works, for those of you who specifically want to run or build communities. Then we take a deeper dive into how to embody each of the Orchestrated Connecting principles yourself for those of you simply looking to engage your personal network in a more purposeful way.

This book will teach you, most importantly, that you already know a lot of what to do and that you should trust yourself more in doing it. It should also be clear that many of the lessons learned in nearly a decade of developing and running the OC community (David) and teaching business students about networks and networking (Noah) are not always shared with the intention of teaching something new but, rather, to reframe and systemize what you might already do instinctively. You can then do these things more purposefully.

It won't be easy, because you will need to start putting these principles into place in your life to truly understand the benefits they provide. But, in doing so, you will better define your purpose, hone your relational skills, and, most importantly, lean into helping others.

With this book, we hope you will find success and purpose in leading a more active, engaging, and powerful life through the relationships that nurture you, your family, your work, and your ambitions. Most importantly, we hope this book will help you create a stronger sense of purpose for the time you spend on this planet.

PART I

Community, Connection, and Orchestrating Your Relationships

You may be just starting to think about your career, nearing the end of it, or find yourself somewhere in the messy middle, but, at some point along your way, you have met someone—hopefully more than one—who has heard and understood you. You likely found it easy to build trust and connect with them. The relevance and value of that connection was immediately obvious. They fell easily into your community.

Other connections may not have seemed all that relevant or meaningful at first. Nothing came from an initial introduction, or even a second interaction, and then weeks or a month passed...

And then something changed. Suddenly, because of one of those interactions, you found yourself at the right dinner party, with the right job, or across from the right person. This is the power of connection and of understanding that community exists around you and around each new person you meet.

1

"You're Invited!": A Community-Building Event

In September 2022, Sarah Joseph received a text from her friend Josh:

> "I have something amazing for you to attend just outside the city in a couple of weeks. A community of connectors (like us). It'll be dope, and, just trust me, you are one of the two people out of our entire friend group who belongs here. Here's a link."

Sarah quickly replied:

> "Ok :] LOL. I'm free that Wednesday so I'll go. But I have to ask, why just me and one other?"

The unusual response gave her pause:

> "Because I'd trust that I could leave the founder's kids with you.

That's the bar for anyone who any of us wants to bring in."

Now Sarah was intrigued, if a little mystified. She didn't have kids. She didn't necessarily want to watch anyone else's, either. But the specificity resonated.

A few weeks passed. The Friday before the event, Sarah received an email welcoming her and the other attendees. Somewhat perplexingly, it provided no indication of who else was coming, who might be speaking, or who would be hosting. It thanked the recipients for their openness to attending, showing up with the curiosity of connection, and the desire to deepen their purpose.

Sarah was drawn in by the clarity of the event's "why," but there also seemed to be a complete lack of logistical clarity—secrecy, even.

Then came the rules. "Rules?" she thought, growing skeptical.

All attendees are required to (a) arrive on time (7:00 p.m.) or text the founder, David, if running late; and (b) attend the entire two-hour event, from start to finish. Food would be served, friendly to many dietary preferences and restrictions. Dress was business casual. The address and first name of the host were not to be shared under any circumstance with anyone else, even if they said they would also be attending.

Clearly, there was a method to this madness. Sarah just wasn't yet sure what it was.

Monday rolled around, and Sarah received a variation of the same email, reiterating everything she'd been told. The Wednesday of the event, Sarah was informed that she would be in Group G, which she would join immediately upon arrival. The members of each group would be answering a series of questions provided by author Gregory Stock, an OC community member. These were the questions for Sarah and her group to answer:

1. Would you be happier with more control over what happens in your life or more control over your response to what happens? How could you gain more of such control?

2. If you had to tattoo your arm with a message to yourself, what would you write?

3. If you could gain any one ability or quality you admire in someone else, what would you choose? Do you think you could develop that ability or quality just by working at it?

Sarah realized that she would be answering these questions with a group of strangers. The introvert in her was nervous. "Plus, what the hell are these questions?" she wondered. But, as the day progressed, her excitement grew—the result of her genuine curiosity and her ruminations on the questions.

Event Orchestration

Before we continue with Sarah's story, it is important to note the crucial elements that go into the orchestration of an Orchestrated Connecting event. A lot of thought goes into the design and advance communication. A huge part of what makes the methodology unique is, simply put, stating the obvious in a systematic way.

Events should be attended for the full duration: people who intend to "drop by" do not have the same intent as those who agree to attend fully. People are reassured when expectations for their mindset and approach—their "why"—are laid out in advance. They know why they, and everyone else, are coming. Some information is omitted, such as speakers' and other attendees' names. This ensures no one will be there simply angling to meet someone specific. Attendees are not going to a particular host's home, because those events, like events with a notable guest speaker, become about one person rather than the community. Such events have their place. This is not it.

The final preparatory information includes the groups and the questions. Sarah, like all attendees, was coming with a mandate to meet a specific but unknown group of people, and to think deeply about her own opportunity to share. The questions have nothing to do with attendees' surnames, occupations, wealth, power, or fame, but, rather, things core to who they really are.

Walking into the event at 6:57 p.m., Sarah noted that nearly all thirty-five attendees were already there. She was welcomed by David and the other early arrivals, and everyone was directed to their group. By 7:01, the event was 100 percent full, with two apologetic people having rushed in with explanations of delayed trains and a slow elevator.

Like many people attending an unfamiliar event, Sarah would typically have shown up and started searching the room for a familiar face. This time, she spied two acquaintances in other groups, but grabbed food quickly and sat down on a couch with a young Black woman and an older Asian man. Facing them on the couch, seated in chairs, were a White woman in her 50s and a young-ish White man. But the diversity was less striking than the energy.

Within minutes, Sarah had learned things about the four strangers in Group G that she was pretty sure she didn't know about most of her closest friends. In the process, she'd somehow managed to share things at a similar level of depth about herself. When and how they transitioned from answering those three questions to describing, in detail, each of the causes that kept them up at night was a bit unclear. Within twenty-five minutes, the five of them had bonded. She knew their names, about their children, and also their fears.

That is how it started.

Thirty minutes into the evening, David walked around the room, informing the groups that it was time to start the official "welcome and presentations" part of the evening.

Sarah, like her group members, didn't want to stop. She thought, "Who builds connection this quickly! How was a group of strangers each able to focus on one another, and not themselves, and still share so much of themselves in the process?"

They kept talking. Finally, at the third nudge, she and her group stood up and moved to hear David welcome the group.

Resonance and Silence

The aim in each gathering or event is to create something with depth. Authenticity. Purpose. Through a specific structure and flow—just like a piece of music that has a form and flow to it—

one can find ways to bring people together to not just "gather" but to artfully join in greater consciousness, subtly and with clarity.

When you finish an Orchestrated Connecting event, we want you to sit, in silence, your mind swirling with the connections you made and all the possibilities in front of you.

This is the same intent David has as a composer. What he aims for from the audience after the last chord is played isn't immediate applause—it's silence. By creating such introspection in each listener's journey, composers can elevate the entire audience because they had a shared experience.

This element is central to the Orchestrated Connecting experience. Building that "resonance" within each group interaction *and* the collective is key. That is why the event design is based on a flow that builds new relationships from the beginning and gives everyone an opportunity to share their voice immediately, regardless of the day they are having or the type of person they are.

Inclusive Event Design

Event design, particularly for traditional networking events, typically caters to extroverts. Those who can walk into a room and strike up a conversation with people they know and also those they just met. In fact, research suggests that people who know and like each other prior to showing up at a mixer are 99 percent more likely to interact at that mixer than are two people who do not know each other at all. In that sense, "mixers" are actually more like "remixers." People stand in groups of comfort, often with those who look like them or with those with whom they can more easily start "small talk." A symphony, it is not.

While, for some, simply having been invited to the same event by a known host may remove any reservation about approaching others at that event, the lived experience of attending small gatherings suggests it may not be that simple. However, by eliminating small talk and putting people in groups immediately, introverts and extroverts comingle. The barriers that typically keep people from meeting someone new—nothing to talk about, awkwardness of small talk, having a bad day, stress about saying the wrong thing, or any variation of a psyche that would make someone feel unwelcome—are essentially removed. With the anxieties of interaction with strangers significantly diminished, each attendee now has a voice from start to finish, and an opportunity to be heard.

With everyone on time and ready to interact, the groups are diversely curated to help everyone engage in building new relationships. Each group includes people of varying ages, genders, and demographic backgrounds, with a focus on those who likely don't know each other, or could discover more depth, in addition to a thoughtful mapping of their passions and interests to maximize potential support of each other. The established flow then promotes richness.

Standing against the back of the couch in the large living room where David welcomed everyone, Sarah couldn't help but feel like she belonged. She had just spent thirty minutes sharing who she was—and having others share with her—in a way that she had rarely experienced. David's description of "connection" caught her attention and refocused her: he shared a story of having realized there were quite a lot of people who had tremendous relationship value that hadn't been valued. That hit home.

David shared the mistakes and realizations he had made that led to the creation and evolution of Orchestrated Connecting:

> "Despite years of helping others, when it came time to look for a new job, so many of the people I thought would be helpful didn't call back, let alone offer to help. People wouldn't recommend me for a position I was qualified for or take a meeting with me. Many who did thought I was in the room to help them again. I had not demonstrated the value I had given to hundreds of others, and they didn't see me as someone who was also in need. Or I may have helped a ton of people who had no interest in ever helping me back. They made me feel like my skill as a connector wasn't valuable—all the while, they kept asking me to make introductions and help them."

Sarah, long believing that her ability to connect was simply a "nice-to-have," started to realize it was likely much more than that. Then, she, along with everyone else in the room, was given permission to ask with purpose and specificity for what she wanted, despite the fact that it was probably difficult for her and everyone else in the room to actually do so.

As David observed:

> "I came to realize that real connectors suck at asking for themselves. Most people do. We are more comfortable asking to support someone else than stating our need because it feels selfish. This is a community where we want you to ask with purpose for what you need and to know everyone is receptive to hear and see how they can support. Truly support."

"I was blown away," Sarah recalls. "This wasn't an event that I was attending in order to help people. It was an event intended to help me accept that it's OK to ask for what I need—almost the exact opposite of what I was expecting." She paused to realize she had bonded with a group of strangers without being asked for a single thing in return.

As this was washing over her, David asked two people to step up to speak in succession. Neither was an event sponsor—there were no sponsors. Each person was invited to practice the Orchestrated Connecting "impact ask": to share their passion and how, specifically, it could be amplified by the people in the room.

A woman stood up first and spoke about her passion for mental health; building community around a specific disorder that was rarely diagnosed properly, and with such stigma that people shied away from speaking about it. Then she spoke about the fact that this affects CEOs, politicians, and millions of people despite most people not knowing anything about it. She closed her eyes suddenly, pausing for twenty seconds, further drawing in the interest of the rest of the attendees, and then went about asking for specific types of people who could align themselves with her mission.

The next speaker? Zak Williams, son of the late actor Robin Williams. Zak is an avid mental health advocate and entrepreneur whose business, built with his wife Olivia, was created in deep alignment with his purpose.

He made his case:

> "I built [PYM] Prepare Your Mind with the understanding that our gut health and our mental health are directly tied, and that, by supporting positive habits to improve our brain health, and our moods, anxieties, and overall feelings, we can learn to bet-

ter control and activate the best parts of our mental health. I'm looking to amplify our product into larger chains, such as Target, or with distributors who want to prioritize health and wellness from a holistic perspective, as well as individuals who want to invest in the future of mental health and healthy supplements and diets."

After each speaker made their impact ask, David prompted them with this question: "What relationships and connections do you need to move your vision forward?" Sarah had several people immediately come to mind while the first woman spoke, and, by the time Zak finished, she was ready to rush up and offer support herself. There would be time for that later. David thanked both attendees for sharing their passions.

Itching to offer introductions, Sarah listened as David explained the only OC community rule—*honoring the chain of connections*—and the "why" behind it. Simply put, should anything materialize as a result of the connections made that evening, the people responsible for making the introductions happen must be thanked.

As David finished, he made a request to all in attendance. Besides finishing the food and drink—no waste!—everyone was asked to go and meet someone new and not just ask with purpose for what they need but to approach those new people as an advocate for the others in their initial groups as well.

The room exploded with energy.

Elevating the Room

Building the right mindset in the room is vital to truly achieving the purpose of an event. It is not only about bringing people together and making sure they have a good time. It is not about the food or the space. It is about designing a safe container where people can share themselves and have the space for others to do the same. The idea is to quickly feel that the time spent is valuable for all.

The first two half-hour blocks of an Orchestrated Connecting event are designed with this specific end in mind: to be welcomed into small, purposeful groups, and then to be shown each attendee's value in coming. That, balanced with hearing similarly purpose-filled people describe projects that relationships can propel, helps set the tone. The final component, the closing reminder to "honor" those responsible for making introductions happen, demonstrates the same value they themselves would hope to have honored when they are the "originator" in a chain of connections.

That is the end of the structured time. The rest is up to the attendees and the energy created by the first part of the evening. It is the freedom and curated "haphazardness" of the second half of the event that allow for real connections to be made. The event intentionally runs for another full hour.

During the second half of the event, Sarah met seven new people in one-on-one or small-group conversations. Twice, she got pulled into conversations by someone she had met earlier in the evening in order to be introduced to yet another new person. In a whirlwind of two hours, her energy had changed from tired but excited to sociable and purposeful.

"I typically leave most social gatherings pretty drained," says Sarah, "but this was not that. Meaningful connection with a handful of people in that context was far more energizing than exhausting. I left counting the number of calls, meetings, or follow-up emails that were going to come out of this."

Sarah finally left at 9:15 p.m. Ready to go home, she found a dozen people talking in front of the host's building. None was ready to leave: mostly strangers but—now she saw clearly—brought together by a defining purpose. Each person belonged.

Sarah walked to the train with someone she hadn't yet met.

She had been reticent to ask for what she needed, preferring to support others during her first gathering, but, when asked this time, she told them she was launching a new start-up focused on financial literacy, helping working-class families teach their kids how to save for their future. Her new "friend" immediately knew an investor to talk to.

In a matter of minutes, they set a coffee meeting for a few days later.

The next day, a follow-up email from David arrived, thanking everyone for joining, recounting the speakers' impact asks, and connecting everyone who attended via email. It encouraged everyone to practice what they did that evening in all their interactions.

And that, Sarah did. A few days later, both she and her new friend showed up early for their coffee meeting in order to get a table and order before the line got too long. They happened upon each other in line and realized they had saved tables right next to each other. Sarah was then invited to a new founder event focused exactly on what she needed to learn, and that catalyzing connection led to new friendships and landed her an investor five months later. She had no idea that would have even been possible until she built relationships without the goal in mind, and ended up with the right outcome anyway.

Purposeful Design

The magic of an Orchestrated Connecting event isn't magic. It's purposeful design. It is, of course, the people who make the difference—and especially the way the people engage with the structure. This is why you go to an event: the hope you will meet someone new and exciting and have at least one decent conversation.

No one expects every conversation to be fascinating. No one expects to have an event where the ROI is all the people they meet offering to "give and support them." No one expects to have a follow-up with everyone. Yet, the OC community onboarding process and the values of the group—being for action-oriented, natural givers—means that even the busiest people always follow up. And, with this, they often share the sentiment and outcome of that interaction.

Behind the scenes, David also tracks action. People who attend and don't follow up on the promises they make are given a chance to do so. And, if they don't, they don't come back. There is a responsibility taken to be part of this group, one communicated in advance of each event and as the mandate in the follow-up.

Sarah's experience is nearly identical to that of every OC member who attends an event. And, while the responses and reactions of each community member are different, the event design—the "ritual"—creates the purposeful community, which is both individual and community driven. When everyone feels a personal connection to the community and sees value in their own role in it, each event reinforces the "groupness" as it welcomes in new individuals to a culture and collective energy that is greater than one can achieve alone.

It is through these kinds of connections that organic community is built. And the OC community is built with the goal of doing it on a grand scale. At the time of writing, the community is 2,000 people strong, scattered across thirty-five countries. Imagine the potential of a community of this size and with this orientation.

2

A Blueprint for Community

—————

Orchestrated Connecting is a values- and purpose-driven community. It comprises a community leader and community members who are themselves "connectors." There is a process to becoming a community member, but, before you toss this whole idea aside as some kind of elitist enclave, hear us out. Community members are nominated or invited to join because of their shared value system, not because of pedigree, education, or job title. There is no membership, no fees, nor any other requirements, other than to lean in and live by the set of shared values, which includes taking part in the regular rituals that come about through events—in person or virtually—that signify "This is a community" as much as the values do. Unified by those values, the rituals, and a desire to contribute to *the community* by helping others within it, the OC community has generated countless success stories and had real, measurable positive impact on the world.

"Welcome In": Inclusion, Opportunity, and Acceptance

> I want to meet all current and future connectors who
> are action-oriented, natural givers—and with whom I
> would be willing to leave my kids.
>
> **—DAVID HOMAN, OC COMMUNITY FOUNDER**

At the heart of any robust community are its leaders and the structural frameworks they impart and reinforce. Whether it's a communal system like a kibbutz, or another collective, a community's strength is amplified when its central figures have clear parameters for engagement.

In particular, community requires boundaries and an initial force that binds the people within those boundaries, both of which often become the foundation for the culture of that community. Historically, these boundaries and forces included things like the need for survival, kinship, shared enemies, and geographic circumstances. In our modern, hyper-connected world, where many of us are fortunate enough to have our basic needs met and daily survival is taken for granted, these forces tend to be higher order: things like identity, purpose, values, and ideology create and bind groups of individuals. In our experience of creating and reinforcing boundaries, a set of positive rules enhances the integrity of the community, defines the values and membership, and creates easy means for reinforcement. By reinforcing the rules as a motivating factor for engagement, community is catalyzed.

The OC community's values and their importance are underscored from the very beginning. To join, it is mandatory that you first meet the founder. This meeting is not about judging worthiness but about gauging alignment of values. Just as important, however, is clearly and intentionally defining your needs. What do you *truly* care about? What gets you out of bed every morning and keeps you awake at night? In walking through this clarification exercise, you—the potential community member—receive your first introduction to two of the community's critical values: clarity and specificity. We elaborate on these below.

Their purpose is not only to make it easier for others to help you as a community member but also to prompt you to crystalize your own thinking so that making a compelling "elevator pitch" (i.e., the impact ask) is substantially easier. Why? It is easier for others to help you when you are clear about your purpose and your needs.

The introductory meeting therefore provides a benefit even if your needs are not met instantly through introductions: achieving clarity around your own impact ask and taking the step to actually ask for what you need. Armed with that clarity, it then becomes easier to find the best connections to make within the OC community. The positive rules and process around community onboarding and participation encourage you to step up, to ask for what you need, and to agree to the values set forth.

After your initial meeting, you are sent the "mantra"—the quote that opened this section above—along with a rule system ("Orchestrated Connecting agreement," shared later in this chapter), and asked to follow up. People who are naturally inclined to give often have a hard time asking for themselves, and we have found that, when people demonstrate an ability to ask with purpose for their needs, their engagement in community is much stronger. The follow-up is the opportunity to make that ask. As "action orientation" is an essential trait for members, the act of following up is a critical signal of an ability to contribute to the community's culture. If you follow up, you are welcomed in.

The OC community rules around empowering people to engage are simple, both for how you "stay in" and how this positive framework helps you. To remain an OC community member, you commit to the rituals and values and you make asks around your passions and purpose. Critically, you also agree to help others when asked. It is, after all, a community of well-networked connectors, and the rules ensure that community members have high integrity. To reiterate, this is not some elitist community of celebrities and high-net-worth individuals (though both do exist among the community members). It is a community of those who find purpose in other communities, manage their own substantial networks, and juggle connections in multiple industries. Members often comment that they are often the most connected person they know, which, ironically, can make them feel lonely or like they are not fully invested in one particular group.

But that position is a strength in the OC network, and therein lies the difference that makes any community special: it brings together people who felt as though, in one way or another, they were outsiders or not fully engaged in other community settings. They finally feel at home among others who share the values that they had difficulty finding elsewhere. For OC members, there wasn't a community for them, yet they understood the power of community and resorted to building their own to meet those needs.

If you want to build a community in which all members benefit, it needs to be populated with an engaged group of members, and the culture must hold a set of shared, rigorously enforced and reinforced values. A single opportunist in a group has the potential to make maintaining a generous culture challenging.

For instance, years ago, an OC member showed up at an event and immediately interrupted a conversation between David and another community member to ask who was "important" that they "should meet." This person then proceeded to "work the room," and, in a stereotypically extroverted, charming way, managed to connect with a few people and exchange numbers. Three months later, a friend in venture capital called David to let him know that his firm had invested in this guy's business. Not only that, but two people in the OC community convinced their friends to co-invest, too—but those two people were never told about the investment opportunity or the outcome. Yet, they had been the ones who had made introductions that led to the deal.

The opportunistic member was pressed as to why the chain of connections wasn't honored. Why hadn't anyone been thanked, or even merely informed, as all it would have taken was a note or a call of thanks for helping make the introductions that made the deal happen? The response was "my project is important, so people *should've* invested." The opportunist's response destroyed the trust that community members had in him. Needless to say, he's now a former OC member.

"You're Out": Values, Equity, and Accountability

At the heart of the Orchestrated Connecting system is a motivating ethos responsible for generating a strong culture. To some extent, the ethos is reminiscent of age-old tribal systems wherein the fear of being ousted from one's primary group acted as a deterrent against undesired behaviors. Community leaders have a twofold responsibility in this dynamic: they must not only exemplify the expected behaviors but also ensure their enforcement.

The absence of repercussions—such as the threat of losing one's place in the community—paves the way for exploiters and opportunists. A community's giving-oriented culture, while commendable, can unfortunately become a breeding ground for selfishness. Generosity often finds itself met with lowest-common-denominator behavior.

Taking Repercussions Seriously

A former OC member was heavily vetted as he came into the community; he was known to a few of David's closest friends and an important investor. At an event early in the existence of Orchestrated Connecting, this individual, whom we will call "Drake" (David knows a lot of people, but no one named Drake), was seen chatting closely with some of the women present. It was all done in what seemed to be a mutually acceptable way. In a safe, contained environment like OC, people let down their guard, assuming the best in others. And, while attraction does occur, the ask is that you ask for their information and follow up the next day.

Nearing the end of the night, Drake met an incredibly dynamic former actress named "Sally" (David also doesn't know anyone called Sally). What began as a fascinating talk about life and work and shared interests evolved into a drink post-event at the bar nearby.

When David received a text the next day from Sally, he was shocked. Though nothing truly horrible had happened to her, she had felt threatened and confused at the end of the night based on how forceful Drake was about her going home with him. David asked Drake to talk, explaining that he was concerned based on what he heard from Sally and wanted to hear Drake's experience.

During that conversation, Drake was, to put it bluntly, a dick. Yelling at David, Drake accused him of taking

Sally's side. David stayed neutral, explaining that, in his opt-in community, he cares about intention and wanted to understand what had happened from Drake's perspective. He and Sally had hit it off and gone out for a private drink after. They had been flirting with each other a bit during the event, so this was not a one-sided engagement.

Drake calmed down but refused to accept that Sally had felt so uncomfortable that she messaged David about it. He declined to say anything beyond reiterating his own perspective, even with a chance to simply acknowledge Sally's, whether he felt her feelings were warranted or not. With that reaction, he sealed his fate in the OC community.

David called the two friends who knew Drake well and confidentially asked them to tell him if Drake had exhibited this behavior before. Both expressed immediate remorse, asking about Sally. One of them offered to call her to apologize and see if she was OK. The other offered to call Drake and talk it out with him. Neither blamed Sally for "leading Drake on." They both asked about her welfare. And Drake was a trusted friend to both of them.

We live in a world where judging whether or not to "make a move" is confusing. Impossible sometimes. However, our actions speak louder than words. Drake chose not to act with empathy, principles, or understanding when it came to owning his part in the situation. Sally did. She reached out confidentially. She recognized her part of their rapport. She acknowledged that they mutually agreed to go out for a drink. But, when she drew a line and asked to leave separately, Drake became more emphatic and later refused to acknowledge anything had happened.

If Drake had apologized, he would've shown his ability to see beyond his own perspective. Instead, he showed character traits not suitable for the Orchestrated Connecting culture. David does not insist, nor even ask, everyone to be a saint in every part of their everyday life. The ask is that certain ethical behavior be adhered to in his community, at his events, and in the interactions that stem from the events. If not, you're out.

♩ ♩ ♩

Robust groups and communities rigorously guard their boundaries, be it in terms of communication protocols, etiquette, onboarding processes, or—perhaps most importantly—upholding core values. The collective understanding here is clear: if a member commits to a set of rules but fails to abide by them, their actions take center stage in the evaluation of their reputation. And, in such a well-defined environment, there's little room for ambiguity or double standards. Everyone operates on the same playing field, ensuring fairness, equity, and equality. Think of the cynicism that would form in a religious community if it were revealed that the spiritual leader was engaging in behaviors that ran directly in opposition to those expected or dictated to the community. Even in a community in which members' power differences in the real world vary significantly, within this space, every member stands equal in the expectations of their relationship value.

"Relationship value," to us, is the most underappreciated commodity we know. It is the social capital that exists between two individuals, creating a trust that is maintained by both sides, positively, to support each other's growth and needs. While it is something that we put a lot of our time and money into, society doesn't tend to value it as much as it should. Nevertheless, it is the building block of purposeful community.

The emphasis on quality is critical. But we're not talking about the quality of someone's résumé or even necessarily of their network. It's the quality of their character vis-à-vis the community's expectations. Someone who continually makes introductions to individuals who don't match the community's expected values jeopardizes their standing. If such introductions persist, the member's role within the group comes under scrutiny, or they face removal. The foundation of this community rests on high-grade, impactful introductions. In essence, the quality of one's introductions not only reflects their discernment but also their commitment to the collective good. After all, your own network is likely your most easily shared and broadly relevant asset.

For Orchestrated Connecting, while members can opt in or opt out based on their preference, over thirty have been removed because of their actions—and this is mentioned at each event, to ensure people know the ethical code is taken seriously.

It's clearly written in the mantra with membership onboarding: *I want to meet all current and future connectors who are action-oriented, natural givers, and with whom I would be willing to leave my kids.* It's said at every Orchestrated Connecting event to establish a code for the type of people we want engaged around us.

Actions, Not Words

In the OC community, commitment is measured by action—follow-through on one's promises. We see four ways in which action is demonstrated: (1) engagement through action, (2) reputation through connection, (3) inclusive value system, and (4) reciprocal benefits.

Engagement Through Action

Your level of engagement determines your stature in the OC community. Responding to David's initial prompt with a clear impact ask and attending Orchestrated Connecting events are markers of active participation. Absence of such actions signifies a lapse in commitment.

Reputation Through Connection

A connector's value is based on the quality of their asks and introductions. In the OC community, ambiguity around reputation doesn't exist. You either add value by fostering connections or you don't.

Inclusive Value System

The community thrives on two key actions: (1) opting in and (2) making introductions. Membership isn't based on superficial merits like appearance, connections, or achievements. Instead, it's determined by proactive contributions toward building relationships. Though all are welcome to join, the OC community is focused on building a group that looks like the year 2040 today, with a focus on maintaining a majority minority community as much as possible. This means that we recognize the difference between the world's population and its breakdown by gender, age, and race or religion as something different than the actual power dynamics that currently exist. Another way to say this is that power is not currently held in any representation for the demographic breakdown of the world or what it will be in the future.

Reciprocal Benefits

The more you invest in the community by aiding others, the more assistance you receive in return *from the community*, not necessarily the individual(s) you help. This dynamic is more than just a transaction; it's a psychological response. Being in an environment of givers with clear purposes and shared values amplifies the urge to give, creating a self-sustaining cycle of growth. The psychological and neurochemical rewards for assisting others (likely driven by dopamine release) further reinforce this giving behavior.

Community Rules

Orchestrated Connecting Agreement

I promise to be honest and to uphold the moral obligations laid forth below, or I will not be allowed to interact in this private circle of individuals without first re-proving my ability to follow these rules.

1. I will only use "double opt-in" to connect individuals, which means both sides must agree to the introduction before it is made.
2. If I offer to make a connection, I will do so without having to be chased down by the person I offered to help.
3. If a person I was connected to helps me, I will credit the person/people who connected me and do everything in my power to keep them in the conversation, where/when relevant.
4. Should a financial transaction occur as the result of connections, I will endeavor to reach out to the individual(s) who connected me and either formalize the relationship or return the favor in a manner that seems to be fair to all parties.

5. I will show up on time to meetings or calls and not cancel without valid reasons.
6. I will respond to any introduction made within two days, even just to inform the individual that I am unable to respond more fully until a later date—no exceptions, except life/family emergencies.
7. I will, at all times, keep the contact information and knowledge of my colleagues' connections private unless I have their permission to share that information.
8. I agree to credit this Orchestrated Connecting gathering as a catalyst for future contacts made from it.

Risk: If two OC members don't uphold the agreement to "honor the chain of connections" (i.e., rules 3 and 4, above), both are removed from the group.

Protective Rules

In a community of action-oriented givers, even with clearly stated values and an accepted agreement, there is still the risk of someone taking advantage of a member's extensive connectivity. Therefore, in the OC community, additional expectations are put in place to protect against such opportunism.

First, members are encouraged to make a maximum of three connections for someone else, and then the other party must (a) make a valuable introduction in return; (b) offer specific, helpful assistance; (c) do either of those two for someone else in the community; or (d) follow up within two weeks with how the introductions have gone, who has responded, and what is happening.

If there is radio silence, a single reminder is issued, and, if there is still no response, the member helping make the introductions is encouraged to stop helping.

Second, if someone in the community wants another member's help, they should be asked to provide a short email about what they need and why. If they're not prepared to do that, they aren't really prepared to be helped.

Third, if a community member doesn't make a meeting that was agreed to and doesn't explain why, they should be asked. If they give an excuse that falls outside the realm of "urgent," the person who was "ghosted" should not give more than one additional opportunity to the other community member.

"You Choose"

This need not be specifically your value system. Nor do you have to form a community to have a value- or rule-based system for how you want to interact. Our point is that, for the OC community and our blueprint, the system applies to those who choose to accept that system and adhere to it.

While some of you reading this may find much of it to be overly prescribed, particularly stringent, or some combination of the two, keep in mind that everything surrounding this community—and the community you will ultimately build—is "opt in." That means, if it's too much for someone, they can choose not to participate. Letting someone in who does not want to abide by such values means everyone else in the community is at risk of being taken advantage of. We do our best to mitigate that risk.

The OC community might appear straightforward—albeit strict in its rules and guidelines—at first glance, but it is intricately designed, merging psychology and sociology with a purpose-driven approach to deliver impact at the individual scale and well beyond. "Purpose driven" implies an intention to accomplish something greater than for just one's own needs. Building a community rooted in diversity and unified by a shared purpose achieves something far greater than one person and their needs. This sense of purpose hinges on taking deliberate steps and taking them actively. Anyone can do it. However, to genuinely spark others' passions and draw people toward a cause, you must raise your voice and be an ardent advocate.

Moreover, incorporating an element of risk makes the community's objectives more captivating, encouraging resonance with others and getting them to join the cause. "Risk" in this case means that, unless you model the expected norms of a community, you are no longer allowed to be in the community (i.e., as noted at the end of the Orchestrated Connecting agreement, shared earlier in this chapter).

Leading or simply being a part of such a community demands a consistent commitment to its ethical principles. While perfection is not the expectation, the intention to uphold these principles cannot waver.

The journey of building and being part of transformative communities is also a journey of self-awareness. You must work to understand your purpose, the communities you belong to (or want to belong to), and the subsequent steps in your personal evolution—that is, your own self-awareness journey. Reading this book is a step toward each of those things—looking forward—not a validation or critique of where you are right now.

3

Finding *Your* Melody

---

efore you can figure out where you belong and which communities to join, you have to be clear on your purpose. You cannot conduct your symphony unless you first master your instrument. As you will discover throughout this book, it is quite challenging to "orchestrate your life" if you haven't spent time figuring out your "melody"—namely, your purpose. In musical terms, a melody is a string of notes that, when heard in a sequence, brings and gives a sense of harmony. Each melody is unique but parts of it can be shared with or similar to others and their melodies. What, then, do we mean by "purpose"?

What gets you out of bed in the morning? What do you do, or want to do, that contributes to something bigger than yourself? This, simply put, is your purpose. It doesn't have to be saving the planet—though that's an admirable purpose—but it does need to be something beyond or outside of yourself.

The concept of purpose is simple enough, but clarifying yours—and then actually doing something about it—is substantially harder. However, there's also some good news about doing the hard work of identifying your purpose: in addition to the intrinsic motivation your purpose provides, it is also a primary driver of job/career satisfaction. And that is just the tip of the iceberg as far as the benefits of having clearly defined your purpose.

According to research exploring subjective well-being across 166 countries and more than 1.7 million respondents, life meaning—measured by asking respondents whether they feel their "life has an important purpose or meaning ('1' = yes, '0' = no)"—was correlated with higher subjective well-being pretty much everywhere in the world. Said differently, regardless of where you live, people who feel a sense of purpose have greater life satisfaction, feel happier, and experience less negative affect. Having a purpose has also been shown to reduce the impact of stress—both emotionally and physically—possibly because purpose carries with it a reserve of positivity that helps provide resilience.

This shouldn't discourage you if you don't yet have a purpose (or several purposes). Rather, it should hopefully motivate you to do the work necessary to identify one and start living it.

Your passion and purpose are your melody; strengthen your understanding of it, and your vision becomes clear. You can't form an orchestra while you are still in search of your melody. You have to embrace authenticity and vulnerability to attract those around you who become part of your harmony, the chords in your song. Those are the people who "hear your melody." Once the music is written, your players can play it.

Finding your melody and then expressing it takes challenging self-work and requires you to understand and embrace your self-worth. In the Orchestrated Connecting world, your purpose is highlighted by your "impact ask," where you share your passions and how they can be amplified. Just like an orchestra, each player is there to amplify your vision. Sometimes, other players add to your voice, but each and every one of them enhances who you are.

Mixing metaphors for a moment, another way to think about your purpose is as your Bat Signal. It is the beacon you put out into the world that attracts other people with similar interests, values, and purpose to you. The clearer your signal, the easier it will be to draw the right people into conversation and community.

Unless you are completely fine with a life of solitude (which few of us are), then your "enlightenment" about your own purpose is likely to come from those around you—the people who highlight the things you care most about and amplify your purpose. That is, your purpose is initially defined individually but isn't fully developed until you engage your community. And you can't put your purpose into action without other people.

Unfortunately, many people give up easily on their path or process and are resigned to an unsettled purpose. We have come across two types of people whose purpose escapes them for one reason or another: those leading "lives of quiet desperation" and those who "rage against the dying of the light." There is also a third type of person: those who are purposeful. We dive into the growth pattern toward purpose next, and, in Part III of this book, we dig deeper into the specifics of the process.

The Path to Purposeful

The path toward becoming intentional in one's actions and goals—that is, "purposeful"—is a progression. It is difficult to achieve, and, in fact, many seek it without ever fully attaining it. And that in itself is very much the journey. As far as orchestrating one's life toward purpose, the three groups below are how we see this progression—and where we see many get stuck. This is typically because people tend to end up in their own way as a function of not building the right community to surround and nurture them.

Group 1: People Who Lead "Lives of Quiet Desperation"

People may know this quote from the American naturalist, poet, and philosopher Henry David Thoreau—or, to date your authors, as part of the film *Dead Poets Society*.

We use it because we have encountered many people who seem to talk about what they were "meant to do" or always "wanted to do." But they did not, and do not, achieve these dreams. Perhaps due to life's hurdles, personal doubts, a lack of clear purpose, lack of action, or lack of community, they live "lives of quiet desperation."

There are people who don't take the steps to identify and work toward their purpose, and then there are people who could have achieved this but life got in the way. To work past this, you have to do the work. To immerse yourself in all the details you can find about the "who," "what," "where," "when," and "how" of the thing you are passionate about, in order to maximize opportunities when they materialize.

Success often hinges on recognizing and seizing these right moments. David estimates that each person has perhaps a handful of opportunities in their life to be ready for—when a powerful connection could alter their path. Without preparation or awareness, these crucial moments can pass by, leading to lingering regrets. When driven by purpose, individuals actively search and prepare for such moments, rather than attributing missed opportunities solely to external factors. Those who ultimately thrive grasp the idea that they're not entitled to success, but they can earnestly strive for it.

It's crucial to understand that many in this group don't simply lack purpose or miss opportunities. Some set aside their aspirations to care for an elderly parent or to raise a child due to societal expectations or norms like love, duty, and respect for family. Their silent yearning isn't always about lost dreams but sometimes stems from recognizing the weight of responsibilities and the absence of supportive communities to achieve their dreams.

What about people who regularly talk about what they are going to do, but never seem to do it? They also fall into this category. And those who tell you they will help you with something or introduce you to someone yet, never seem to be able to get around to it? Yep, they, too, fall into this category.

In some cases, there are people in this Thoreau group who simply want more than they can get. They are the Willy Lomans of the world. Willy Loman, from Arthur Miller's play *Death of a Salesman*, is a depressed salesman who never achieved what he wanted to in life. The never-ending yearning for more ultimately kills him.

If you do not stay among the Thoreaus (and, hopefully, don't want to become a Willy Loman type), you will begin to see that a recurring theme among purpose-driven individuals is their emphasis on creating community around themselves. A supportive community can provide resilience during tough times. If this description resonates with you, you're on the path to discovering, or even building, your community.

Group 2: People Who "Rage Against the Dying of the Light"

> Do not go gentle into that good night.
> Rage, rage against the dying of the light.
>
> **—DYLAN THOMAS**

Philosophy and poetry capture the imagination of the human condition. Thomas's famous poem speaks to those whose fire burns deeper. Every night, people who fit into this category head to bed full of passion or brimming with anger about the fact that they do not yet have what they want. They wake up continuing to work on solutions.

Here, "rage" represents an intense drive. It's a positive force when directed toward constructive goals. Our backgrounds and appearances can significantly shape our paths, but our drive to overcome and excel often stems from challenges and a vision beyond personal needs.

This passionate pursuit can manifest in various ways:
- individuals who channel their emotions productively (i.e., those on the path to purposeful)
- some whose intense feelings propel them but might also keep them restless (i.e., those working toward purpose but who may fail)
- those who point fingers and place blame (i.e., the selfish assholes)

How you deal with your emotions around this rage can either fortify your purpose, leading to refreshing mornings filled with renewed energy, or keep you restless, constantly seeking validation and recognition. To rage against your purpose is to believe the world has treated you unfairly because you "deserve" something more than someone else does, and therefore you often place yourself on a hierarchy above others. Ultimately, you find yourself in a position of being a "taker," which you justify to yourself as a consequence of that feeling of deserving something.

Hedge fund manager Ray Dalio, whose son David worked with for several years incubating a film company focused on impact, says this about humility:

> "Humility is as important, or even more important, as having the strengths yourself. Having both is best."

In our experience, if you build community to achieve a larger goal, you act humbly while your "rage" fuels your purpose. If you develop a network to achieve only your purpose, you eventually stand alone. Those who define their purpose and channel their individual needs into a greater cause succeed precisely because that solution builds community.

Group 3: People Who Are Purposeful

The origins of Orchestrated Connecting can be traced back to the influence of NEXUS, a community of social entrepreneurs, next-generation wealth holders, and visionary leaders. NEXUS's impact is likely to be felt over the next several decades, and it is a beacon of purposeful endeavor for global betterment. NEXUS's co-founder Rachel Gerrol is a shining example of someone whose purpose pervades all she does.

Genuine Gratitude, Purposeful Connection

When Rachel was approached to attend the inaugural Orchestrated Connecting event, she responded specifically with her availability: "November 1, 2017." And so it was. Orchestrated Connecting then became a reality, anchored by the magnetic pull of Rachel's reputation. David's vision—his "need" (the roles of *wants*, *desires*, and *needs* in achieving purpose are described in the following section)—was clear: to distill the essence of networks like NEXUS, molding them into his community's blueprint. The ideal participant? An "action-oriented, natural giver" and someone David trusted deeply—so deeply that he would entrust his newborn daughter, Eva, with them.

With a presence in over seventy countries, NEXUS brings together some of the world's most impactful leaders, philanthropists, and change-makers. It is a nonprofit organization, with a clear "no solicitation" policy. While some might seek more from NEXUS, Rachel and her co-founders have crafted a community that caters to genuine needs rather than transient wants. It's a space where co-founder Jonah Wittkamper's ethos resonates profoundly: close your eyes and imagine this group will "support you for the rest of your life."

Yet, fostering such a community goes well beyond merely establishing it and instilling critical values. It entails strategic growth, promoting unity, and sustaining support such that cohesion among its members is foundational. Rachel's approach to managing thousands of various members in NEXUS stands as a testament to this approach.

Amid a constant deluge of requests, she discerns the underlying needs behind every ask, encouraging individuals to channel their passions in a way that also brings others along. For example, when Nobel Peace Prize laureate Malala Yousafzai and her sports enthusiast husband Asser Malik attended the 2023 NEXUS Global Summit, under Rachel's encouragement, they shared their mission to champion girls' empowerment through sports in regions like India and Pakistan. Members of NEXUS rose up together to meet with Malala and Asser to advise and connect them to support their vision.

Rachel acknowledges Orchestrated Connecting's philosophy as being instrumental in her approach—especially regarding genuine gratitude and purposeful connections. It is this ethos that ensures every member in the community understands how to contribute meaningfully.

Achieving Purpose

If you haven't guessed it already, the primary challenge of being either a Thoreau or a Thomas is isolation. When you sit alone with your thoughts or your regrets, you sit alone. Yet, simply being with others is not sufficient either: seeking purpose and trying to get others to bend to your needs is also a path to failure. What, then, can help bring clarity to your purpose in such a way as to enable an organic path to community?

There are three basic sentiments, discussed next, that you must work through to achieve purpose, as well as one primary, overriding practice to put into place.

Wants, Desires, and Needs

Defining these sentiments helps to illustrate the importance of focusing on your true needs as a means of discovering your purpose:

- "Wants" suggest a feeling that one deserves or is owed something—often, something someone else has. Wants are often not critical, but can create an impetus to take something without valuing it. They involve a feeling of something lacking or of scarcity.

- "Desires," at the center of our psyches, are dangerous. They are the deepest feelings of what we want but cannot have. A desire is so urgent it is almost possessive, and we become addicted to the act of taking something and valuing it for having taken it, rather than actually needing it.
- "Needs" are at the core of purpose, because knowing what is essential to us—what motivates us—gives us clarity. What are the things you simply cannot live without? What are the things that are so critical to your being and your view of the world that you feel you have no choice but to pursue them?

When we can understand and communicate our *needs*, that defines our purpose.

The distinction between wants, desires, and needs is often murky, especially as we sometimes use them interchangeably in everyday use. So it's important to look at intentions. Is the outcome primarily for the benefit of the individual or a larger purpose? The following three fictionalized accounts of conference attendances illustrate the differences:

- Evan *wants* to attend a major conference (and not pay). He believes that he deserves to be there, mostly because it will be good for him. His attendance doesn't add any value to the conference, and he likely could have budgeted to attend on his own dime. His ask (to attend the conference for free) is clearly self-centered and not respectful of the conference's goals or its intentions—not to mention the fact it's expensive to run one—but his *want* is based on the value he puts on the experience being greater than the value he will actually give. Evan gets into the conference, pisses off his friend who invited him, and doesn't get invited back.

- Alisha *desires* to meet a very prominent person at the same conference. Her *want* to attend is similar to Evan's, but, in this case, she knows that, if she could only get that moment, the interaction will change her life and career. She pushes hard to get in, and then to move to the front of the line, disrespecting the people also waiting to talk to the same person, ignoring their moments for her own. Her actions are desperate and self-focused, and, even if she gets her chance, she will ruin it because her only goal, her only desire, is for this person to solve something she can't do herself, or to shortcut the hard work others put in because she *has to* have this interaction work. Alisha jumps in front of a group of others to talk to her VIP, ignoring the two people who could have helped her, and ruins her friendship with the person who brought her because her actions reflected poorly on her friend.

- Tolu *needs* to get funding for her start-up. She's spent two years bootstrapping it and knows that, as a female founder, the odds are against her. She built her business to help other women, and the upcoming conference has a focus for founders addressing unmet funding needs. She knows, if she doesn't get funding soon, things will be hard, but she is confident she will find her way. Her positive, purposeful attitude gets her into the conference. At the last minute, a panelist drops, and she ends up on the panel with the VIP she wanted to meet. They grab lunch after. She makes her impact ask succinctly and purposefully and her new friend smiles, as she knows exactly the right person to introduce Tolu to.

This is the difference between purposeful actions and their intentions—and results—and why you must be clear on what you actually need. Purpose-driven needs are those that are most likely to both be fulfilled and to generate broader positive outcomes.

They are also more effective in building and mobilizing community. When you work to achieve a greater vision, it happens because you see the larger picture, and give others sufficient perspective to see what true collaborative effort can create.

Connecting with Purpose to Deliver a Greater Vision

A seminal biopic on the late Congressman John Lewis happened because Ben Arnon and Erika Alexander understood their needs and defined their purpose. Their clarity enabled them to build a purposeful community prior to the "asks" they needed to make to create the film.

John Lewis: Good Trouble came out shortly after the murder of George Floyd in 2020, but it all started two years earlier. Erika and Ben met at the 2008 Democratic National Convention in Denver, where Ben was a delegate for Senator Barack Obama and Erika was a delegate for Senator Hillary Clinton. They had "put in their time" in political activism: Ben had organized Maxine Waters's and Jane Harmon's congressional districts on behalf of the Obama campaign in 2007, while Erika had spent time as a celebrity activist for Clinton, along with John Lewis, Stacey Abrams, and many others.

Ben and Erika had spent years building their community in and around the political and entertainment worlds based on a shared purpose: elevating the stories of social justice warriors. They brought this to reality with their company, and their shared passion for impactful media.

Because of her acting and political work, Lewis's office knew Erika. They knew that she and Ben had launched Color Farm, a production company with a focus on shifting narratives in media through telling bold, inclusive stories on social impact. The company's purpose fit perfectly with John's life story.

Color Farm identified the need for a strong, Black, female director. But, when they approached Dawn Porter, she said she had her own film in development. Each with backgrounds as community organizers, Erika and Ben immediately approached Dawn in the spirit of collaboration. She had an incredible story, while Erika and Ben had Lewis himself, in addition to access to the top politicians in the US. Together, their visions aligned, and the result was greater than each individual project. With Dawn's development deal in place, they were quickly able to engage Participant, Magnolia, and other socially oriented production companies for a massive theatrical release.

Then COVID hit. The world shut down. May 1 passed, and big premieres at the Carter Center, Tribeca Film Festival, the *Time* 100 gala honoring Lewis, and the National Museum of African American History and Culture in Washington, D.C. all got pushed. Only local drive-in movie theaters, where audiences could watch safely from their cars, were able to screen the film. This was no way to build community.

However, the connectors behind the film's production saw an opportunity. Their coalition mindset led them to seek out partnerships with Color of Change, the NAACP, and voting rights groups, as well as corporate partnerships with the NBA and Google, among others. The constraints of COVID-related restrictions yielded an innovative approach to a social impact campaign. It gave a powerful, targeted voice to groups aching for a story of hope in the wake of Floyd's murder and the national recognition of the Black Lives Matter movement.

Though fully virtual, corporations that usually put a few hundred people in a theater to see something "of impact" were buying 60,000 virtual seats to watch online. OC member Emily Best, founder of Seed&Spark, had recently launched Film Forward, a SaaS (software as a service) platform, with the express purpose of bringing films into workplaces for education and social action. Film Forward wraps assessment and surveys as well as guided actions and relevant resources, making it possible not just to demonstrate but also to measure the power of media to change perspectives and compel action.

Connectivity grew as the biopic immortalized the story of one of America's most significant civil rights champions and congressmen. The passing of Congressman Lewis became a call to action from which ripple effects still resonate today.

Erika and Ben did what few do well. They brought together multiple competing voices, all relevant but often working separately. They effectively merged Hollywood and Washington, D.C. They elevated others above themselves and for the greater good. And then they accomplished the true inspiration of this release: they made the viewership of *John Lewis: Good Trouble* purposeful and active. Audiences didn't simply watch and then "feel good." They weren't doing something for social justice by sitting down, eating popcorn, and hearing someone else's story. Instead, they became a more active part of the movement that Erika, Ben, and Dawn have been working on. Their company, Color Farm, is now positioned as a media company with the right access, backing, and skills to continue to change lives over and over again.

Content of Character

A cornerstone of the Orchestrated Connecting philosophy is an emphasis on the "content of character" as a testament to a person's integrity. It transcends superficial distinctions like gender, skin color, or sexual orientation, focusing instead on intent and purpose.

While desires and wants can be consuming, fulfilling true needs brings contentment. If you possess a genuine need that aligns with both self-interest and the greater good, then your desires transition from feelings of frustration and jealousy to a sense of alignment around purpose. It becomes easier to bring others to your cause.

Understanding and embracing your purpose can bridge differences, helping you find your community—ideally, a group aligned on shared values, not demographic characteristics. Recognizing those whose needs and purposes resonate with yours provides a clearer vision for the potential community. Every successful individual we encounter attributes their success to their supportive "village": people who saw their dreams and aspirations as a chance to amplify their own, collectively working toward a shared goal.

Identify Your Purpose

We want you to begin thinking about *your* purpose so that, once you finish this book, you will be able to call upon like-minded individuals to help you amplify it. We offer two exercises to help in this process, the second of which—the *impact ask*—is a cornerstone of the Orchestrated Connecting methodology.

Write Your Obituary

One way to gain clarity into your purpose and values is to sit down and write your own obituary. This is not making a specific commitment to something particular, but offering clarity into what matters to you.

Morbid? *Maybe.* Difficult? *Definitely.*

But it can be an incredibly powerful forcing function to get you to break through the fog of the proximate demands on your time and life to take a larger perspective. Noah asks the undergraduates in his Leadership class to do this exercise, specifically to help these students think through what is meaningful to them as they prepare to embark on their career.

There's no need to show this to anyone; the simple act of doing it can reveal more about what truly matters most to you.

- What meaning did your life have and will you be satisfied with that?
- What accomplishments are really worth noting?
- Did you do anything so regrettable it makes history?
- Do you do anything so positive you wish people truly knew?
- What do you want to be remembered as, by, and by whom?

Your Impact Ask

How do you approach others in the most effective and efficient way to highlight your passions and your needs, while also helping others dream of ways of amplifying them with you?

Givers, in particular, are great at asking for others, but not for themselves. This is why David honed, as part of the Orchestrated Connecting methodology, the impact ask. While you ultimately will use the impact ask to call upon others in the most effective and efficient way to highlight your passions and your needs after you have an idea of your purpose, walking through the exercise below to hone your impact ask can also help clarify your purpose.

It goes like this:

1. What's the impact of a project you're working on? (Hint: Talk about your passions and why the project matters to you, whatever the circumstance.)

2. What happens when that impact is amplified? (Hint: Dream big and get people to see the ripple effect of what happens when what you're doing scales and helps others.)

3. What type of connections do you *need* to move this forward? (Caution: Everyone "fails" this to start with, because they ask for what they *want* or *desire* instead of painting the picture to "trigger" connectivity from others.)

Remember that, when you ask by triggering how what you're doing can fulfill and amplify others, you ask from a position of strength. When you position your ask to paint a broad picture of the type of connection, geography, company/impact/brand, and goals, you can get people to realize the potential of aligning your networks together.

With that, there's more impact, and you've been heard.

Orchestrated Connecting's Impact Ask

Our passion lies in the power of connection, and we want to support more connectors and seek to connect them to one another.

To amplify this vision: we build a larger, more purposeful community that values relationships and no longer feels disconnected or alone. As we expand this community, we will help make "relationship value valued and launch a 'connector economy.'"

And as for the connections we need to move this forward? We'd like to meet people who spend their time making introductions, always seem to know the right person, host the most engaging dinner parties, and never seek fame from those they know, just mutual respect and value. We want to meet founders, investors, community leaders, conveners, people who run conferences, people who run companies, and people who run communities who are committed to helping others philanthropically and with impact at the core of their intentions.

Melody

We began by talking about finding your "melody"—the unique series of notes that make you *you*. When identified and honed, your melody represents your need, your clear purpose. How you sequence each note of your melody and how you share it with the world helps others find their resonance with you. Bringing in others—building harmony and community—amplifies your melody and makes it soar.

4

Purposeful Connecting, Purpose-Driven Communities

The apparent ease of conducting belies the work an individual must undertake to be able to simultaneously hear parts of the whole and how they fit into it. The conductor of an orchestra auditions every member, and those members also police themselves to make sure each section, each soloist, is at their best so that, collectively, they can rise above their individual performances to form a community.

That is all an orchestra is: a community. A community of musicians who agree on the music to be played, the time to play it, who will lead them, and that they are stronger together than apart. And, while they may have guest conductors or soloists come and go, the best orchestras in the world work just the same as the most important communities. They are accepting of others, and they embrace one another's differences because of their collective belief in something "sounding" greater than themselves. The community leader is that conductor, or anyone who brings people together for a shared purpose.

We utilize the term "orchestrating" in the context of bringing all the various parts together. We are all already conductors in our own lives. The work to build your community and tighten the bonds among your "members" is what orchestrating your life is truly about. We can have individual bonds, and bonds shaped by circumstances, but, when you bring your "community" together, then the sum is not just greater than the parts. The collective breadth of those on your wavelength not only strengthens you, it uplifts them too.

Our connections, the interweaving networks of colleagues and friends, play a pivotal role in sculpting our identity, steering our beliefs, values, and even our actions. But it goes deeper than connections. Without a foundation of genuine, *widespread* trust among the people in your network, connections can lack substantive value.

This moves us beyond the concept of a "network," which is primarily interested in your success: assisting you in achieving it and, conceivably, leveraging it. Conversely, a "community" harbors a more profound, holistic interest in support and in your development. While success is inherently a part of development, the latter encapsulates more: growth, purpose, comfort, and vulnerability. These aspects become the bedrock upon which communities are constructed, creating a virtuous cycle—if the community's values are reinforced. It is in these trusted relationships that we find the key to everything.

Recognizing the Value of Purposeful Connecting

Today, OC community member Ramphis Castro is an entrepreneur, philanthropist, venture capitalist, arts lover, father, and visionary in revolutionizing how we tackle childhood poverty. With the successful and influential Platform for Social Impact he helped found, he now works to address and change the cycles of poverty that many of his friends and family have faced back home in Puerto Rico. He was able to overcome them, and, in doing so, he set himself apart from so many in his community.

Ramphis recognized that the systemic change required to address poverty needed government, private investors, philanthropists, and community leaders working together. He and an amazing co-founder, along with many visionary partners, set out to build a solution that would work to alleviate poverty through education, health access, and entrepreneurship. Taking his own journey and clearly defining his needs, he cultivated a purposeful community to change the lives of thousands and eventually serve as an example of how to address this challenge globally.

Ramphis grew up "looking up at the different strata" in his hometown of Guayama, Puerto Rico. Pulled out of school several times because his parents couldn't pay the tuition on time, he often felt alone. However, he also understood that he needed to find a way to get away from the "scarcity mindset" that he grew up with and find a path that would provide access to what he wanted for his life. But no one could really help him. At least not yet.

"I was somehow aware of the inequity inherent in the world," says Ramphis, "and realized there were no natural networks that I felt I would be able to tap into in Puerto Rico that would help me break into the industries that I'd developed an interest in."

Recognizing the need for connections but lacking any, Ramphis believed that he needed the kind of social proof that would signal his value to others; something that could provide a means for accessing the elusive networks that he believed held the potential to level up his career.

So, he set out on a path to achieve that goal. To define and redefine how people saw him. It began with a journey to develop his own skills and strengths and transformed into one to model and create possibilities for others. Here's how he began.

Ramphis majored in computer engineering, made sure to hone his native-level English skills, and got his JD. He got an opportunity to start his career at Microsoft, crediting this break to a series of lucky incidents. Still, he says, "I had the social proof, but there was always a nagging narrative of inadequacy, of not belonging." He pressed on.

Eager to grow his social world and to help others by sharing valuable insights he'd gained from early failures in building his own companies, Ramphis became a member of several new entrepreneurial ecosystems like Techstars and Lean Startup. His appreciation for the opportunities provided by his education and newfound access to networks beyond his hometown and home country informed his approach to developing new relationships:

> "I observed others and came to understand, through experience, the importance of paying it forward, offering support, building trust, and being helpful in practical, tactical ways that

> created value for the network, even if it didn't directly benefit me." What was obvious to Ramphis is often overlooked, under-appreciated, or simply ignored by others.

In retrospect, it is easy to see how and why he has done well for himself, but, because he took a long-term perspective in reaching his goals, it was not immediately clear at the outset whether his process was going to pay off. For example, in 2005, the U.S. Small Business Administration was trying to help economic development in Puerto Rico by focusing on small businesses rather than start-ups. Ramphis didn't think this was necessarily the most effective or valuable approach. Tapping into the robust network he had cultivated in his home country, he reached out to an engineering guild that had connections to governmental services in Puerto Rico. Doing so unlocked opportunities for local start-ups, but it took significant time. As of 2015—ten years after the program launched—there was still very little venture capital investment in Puerto Rico, but, by the end of 2020, that number approached $300 million. The seeds planted over a decade earlier, with connections created even before that, ultimately bore fruit.

Ramphis says:

> "Asking and acting with purpose has changed my whole ecosystem of relationships. I find that it puts those with shared purpose in front of me more and more in a way that is meaningful, actionable, and full of wonderful serendipities each time."

Ramphis lives his life and cultivates his own community via an approach that is strikingly similar to that of the

OC community. He no longer feels he has to go it alone. He now has plenty of people to help.

𝄞 𝄞 𝄞

With Ramphis's story and those of others that we will tell throughout this book, we don't wish to imply that raw intellectual horsepower and grit don't matter. That couldn't be further from the truth. Those qualities are necessary for accomplishing your personal goals and achieving things far greater than yourself. However, they are not sufficient.

Connectivity is the source of amplification and acceleration.

But, as we have found, even connectivity as it is often depicted—for instance, making sure you never eat alone—is not enough, at least not if greater societal impact is your goal. Expanding your network and building your "social capital"—your ability to access and accomplish things based on your connections and their capabilities and connections—are incredible professional levers. We have found this to be the focus of a lot of approaches to networking, whether directly or indirectly.

If much of the current wisdom on networking suggests giving as a means of getting something in return, then helping others under these circumstances is simply a way of stockpiling return favors for yourself some time down the line. Such reciprocity is a powerful motivational and moral force. But, in many ways, this approach can still turn into a kind of instrumental networking, which makes people uneasy. Additionally, how do you know what people need, or even what *you* really need, in order to make such generosity and reciprocity authentic and meaningful?

Eight years ago, when Ramphis joined the OC community, he experienced a radical shift in his perspective, which now focuses on greater intentionality in his network-building; how he manages the people whose visions aligns with his own, but, more than anything, how he engages people in "movements" rather than "networks." This represented a shift from organic growth to more systematic and purposeful community-building. His personal theory of networking was perfectly aligned with that of Orchestrated Connecting, but he is now in a community with hundreds of similarly valued yet still highly diverse individuals who are collectively engaged in a more structured approach to their community.

The immense potential possessed by the OC community has not been achieved through alchemy, some kind of social luck, or individuals each seeking to better themselves via their own networking prowess. It is the intentional result of a fine-tuned and intensely reinforced series of rituals, processes, and rules that sit at the intersection of human behavior and social science.

Orchestrated Connecting isn't the only reason Ramphis has been able to progress in his quest to tackle childhood poverty, but it has very much accelerated the process.

What Do We Mean by "Community"?

We think it's time to reinvent and reinvest in community.

As a species, we have been doing community for thousands and thousands of years. But, in recent times, in many ways, we are moving away from the kind of community that has real, broad power. At the very least, many of us are retrenching into homogenous communities of like-minded others. You don't need to look far to find evidence of online echo chambers, highly specific and tailored cultural offerings, and niche hobbies. People have historically referred to these as "tribes."

Humans' default mode is one of tribalism. It has typically kept us in like-minded (and like-appearance) groups. This approach to gathering while excluding others is universal, giving us the longstanding aphorism "birds of a feather flock together." It is generally accepted social science wisdom that "homophily"—the principle that similar people are drawn to one another—is the primary driver of our interpersonal connections. So it has been for centuries, dividing us along not just demographic lines but socioeconomic, educational, and political lines as well.

The Internet facilitates our ability to find like-minded people, no matter where in the world they may be. And, in some important ways, the divisions and lines between us now are becoming harder to distinguish. The same Internet connectivity that enables homophily to extend beyond your family or hometown also creates opportunities to branch out. Physical borders no longer carry the same weight. While recent world conflicts and epidemics have brought to light just how connected and how tribal we are, society continues to move forward, redefining borders and broadening the potential of global communities. Try as some might to fight it, we are now a global, easily and always connected world.

The opportunity for connection is there, as is the potential for genuine engagement beyond the superficialities of modern networking. Our evolving global community certainly presents a chance to reinforce our existing beliefs, but, more importantly, it offers the opportunity to challenge and expand them.

It's crucial not to overlook the depth and richness that diverse connections can bring. By proactively seeking interactions with individuals from varied backgrounds, professions, and ideologies, we can actively invest in our personal and communal growth.

However, it's a deliberate, sometimes challenging choice to forge connections that aren't just reflections of our current selves but that provide windows into perspectives that can redefine us and our worldview. The power, then, lies in not simply creating connections but in cultivating them with intent, curiosity, and respect. It's here that we transition from mere networking to the establishment of a true, diverse, purpose-driven community.

Our vision of community is a grouping of individuals no longer drawn together by demographic features like faith, country, ideology, or occupation, and instead driven by purpose. Building community requires looking past the easy, visible sources of commonality and maintaining a clear focus on our humanity, as well as a desire to codify that into policy and action—all as a means of making substantive individual and collective change.

While we do not intend to preach or place our values or specific beliefs into this, we do want to acknowledge that not all communities based on shared values or purpose exist for the "greater good." Our studies of many networks, of our history as the human race, and of our tribal natures have shown us that the formations of groups have often been recipes for power grabs that bring out the darker side of humanity. However, we believe that the tenets we lay out here and throughout our analysis of principles and values will work to create communities for which the purpose is not the preservation of a destructive value system but the elevation of all humankind.

The fundamental aspects of community are not demographics but values, rituals, and a sense of belonging. Since the beginning of modern social science, it has been held that, without ritual, there is no society. Rituals bring people together, delineate who and what is important to a collective, and create a sense of oneness among a group of individuals. The interdependence created by the rituals and the oneness is what drives the sense of belonging.

Think of the communities many of us are already a part of (e.g., religious groups, alumni associations, book clubs, sports team fan groups): each is defined by some kind of regular gathering. No gathering, no community.

But, moving beyond the nature of gathering, what kinds of people are involved, and under what circumstances and conditions can we get them in the same place regularly? Furthermore, how can we quickly build trust among them? Shared values and mutual connections will only go so far.

We'll get to these questions. Before that, though, we want to share the story of another individual, Gopal Patel, who sought to build an ambitious, purpose-driven community.

Purpose-Driven Communities

Gopal Patel is the co-founder of Bhumi Global, an environmental organization rooted in Hindu beliefs of the balance between people and the natural world. It represents his first step toward building purposeful community. Gopal is also a TED speaker, intertwining multi-faith and climate change activism in a dance that has inspired tens of thousands of individuals to bridge their faith with fervent climate engagement.

As Gopal walked on the stages and into the rooms filled with global shapers, he began to realize that one community's efforts alone were not enough. He recognized that a balance of power was in the collaboration of faith leaders and practitioners from many walks of life; that our commonality was more strongly rooted in our humanity than in our differences in faith. Faith and climate change activism in particular have had numerous challenges in history, especially around balances of power, but Gopal speaks about, consults in, and leads movements to refocus our faith narratives on the power of needing multiple perspectives.

Born to an Indian mother and an Indian father who was born in Africa, with his roots tracing back to England, and now flourishing in the United States, Gopal embodies a tapestry of multiculturalism. His vision? To bring voices from diverse faiths, primed for individual action, into a united front. A coalition that challenges and collaborates with governments, corporations, religious institutions, and philanthropies, aiming for a world where power dynamics evolve for the collective good.

Gopal has spearheaded the development of environmental initiatives engaging religious communities and their leaders in India, East Africa, Europe, and North America. He has engaged thousands to take positive action toward climate change.

His perception, at the time of writing this, is that his heritage of belonging to many places, intertwined with his faith, has led to a deep belief that we must activate our faith in humankind to achieve the climate solutions we need, and that we cannot divide our society by one faith versus another, but instead cherish the aspects of each that bring us together to heal our climate and allow each faith to serve in their image of where spirituality meets purpose.

While Bhumi Global was the culmination of his vision and needs at the time, Gopal has since moved on to work more broadly with global leaders to harness the power of faith in addressing global challenges. His work continues to recognize that, if the estimated 900 million Hindus, along with other faith communities worldwide, were to take collective action, the world's climate challenges and similarly pressing global issues would be in a much better place.

♩ ♩ ♩

Community builders see where the non-superficial commonalities among people make bringing them together and defining a new, shared purpose worthwhile. They seek to build a new tribe. They realize that, while society may define us in different ways, they have the power to transform shared values into new purposeful groups. They realize they are not alone, and, by doing so, catalyze collective action.

We argue that the elements needed to spur societal-level reconstruction stem from purposeful communities, and that the most progressive societal changes occur because of diversity. Diversity of thought, of age, of heritage, of faith.

While we know this book will not solve the challenges facing our current world, we believe that, if more of us built relationships with integrity—and valued those relationships purposefully—in a more systematic way, the takers among us would become marginalized and have to adapt to the new mainstream.

Purpose-driven communities are for people who wish for more than just a sense of belonging, even if that may ultimately be a positive consequence too. They are for people who want to challenge the status quo by refusing to accept differences as division and choose to congregate around a desire to achieve more.

Though still burgeoning, purpose-driven communities exist because people find others whose content of character is more like theirs. These groups are special: people join them when they feel they share the same values and goals—goals well beyond themselves. Often, people come to them having felt left out or treated poorly in other groups. They've been made to feel different and not welcome, just because they didn't fit the usual mold. Homophily strikes again: tribes, like society more broadly, have reasonably fixed ideas of what's "normal."

But history shows us that brave individuals can change this. They stand up and make a difference for those who've been ignored or mistreated by those in charge. And there is not only safety but power in numbers: when enough people come together for a shared purpose, they can make a big change. This way becomes the "new normal." It's not easy to create these groups. It takes a lot of hard work, determination, and a big idea that everyone can believe in and support.

Change-makers like Gandhi, Martin Luther King, Jr., Nelson Mandela, Malala Yousafzai, Greta Thunberg, and Rosa Parks each stood up to what was "normal" and gave way to a movement that created a new paradigm shift in how we view the world and how we can change it.

Finding Your Community

Community makes achieving and amplifying your purpose easier. Relationships accelerate change, and opening up and sharing your needs with the right community help make it sustainable. Community provides the resilience required to achieve those needs in the face of headwinds and setbacks. Sarah from Chapter 1 saw and felt the potential when she attended her first Orchestrated Connecting event. Each of the following chapters will offer insight into how to do it, and why we think you should too.

We will ask you to think about:

- How would you define the culture of people who surround you?
- How diverse is your network?
- How comfortable are you with truly being vulnerable?

- How often do you actually practice generosity and help others?
- Do you act honorably when you receive help from others?
- Do you go through life with a spirit of curiosity?

PART II

Principles and Core Values

We are encouraging you to find your purpose through both self-reflection and engaging in purposeful community. To do either, you have to trust yourself—embracing your vulnerabilities, taking risks to grow and evolve—and then you have to be courageous enough to help others around you do the same.

Our feeling is that we need a "why now" as much as we need a "how to," and the case for the former is compelling. Despite the increasing ease with which we can connect with people who are far from us geographically, ideologically, and educationally, we feel more and more isolated and lack the skill set and the principles needed to find and connect with like-minded people.

"Like-minded" in this sense does *not* imply an echo chamber. In fact, many like-minded people come together because of their important differences, creating communities that are anything but homogenized or circumstantial.

This maturation of community and the principles that we believe underlie it are the focus of Part II. We know that if you are purposeful, positive, and principled, then collectively we can work to solve challenges, whether global or local, more frequently and with greater depth. Let our approach to connecting and community make the case for reversing the trend of increasing tribalism.

That is *our* "why." And, as we are both also musicians ("musician" is perhaps a generous description of Noah's capabilities), we're here to help make your life, and the lives of those around you, a symphony.

5

Culture

Culture is a set of living relationships working toward a
shared goal. It's not something you are. It's something
you do.

—DANIEL COYLE

You know culture. It's everywhere: the expected behaviors and
mentality of the members of the group. What is allowed and
expected, and what is neither allowed nor welcome, if people
are to remain aligned with the group. A great deal has been written
about culture—what it is, how to build it, its consequences, why it
"works"—and there is general agreement that culture's importance
stems not so much from there being one "good" or "right" culture,
but, rather, that the "best" culture is the one that is best suited for
the context in which the group in question finds itself.

Simply put, the culture of a group of people is most effective
when it is aligned with the goals of that group and when it is
generally consistent in terms of the norms, beliefs, and behaviors
expected of the members of the group.

Sounds simple enough, but let's look at the idea in practice. Many communities, events, conferences, or gatherings will welcome whoever is interested and tell them how amazing they are. But are they? Is the host simply spouting an empty nicety? How were the people there vetted? Were you aware of any principles or guidelines used to inform whether you should choose to participate fully in this group or experience?

The culture of any collective or event that doesn't tell you why you are there, and why others by virtue of that culture are not, has failed to achieve a higher purpose. Yes, failed. And, while it is not necessary to dictate every behavior, norm, and selection criteria of a group, it is important to create the standards and expectations for people to gather.

Let's take a Monday Night Football gathering as a simple example. The organizer of the meet-up sets the expectations. You may not all be rooting for the same team, but you and the others in attendance are there to watch the game. And, while it is most often left unsaid, as someone in attendance, you are also among those that the organizer (or a friend) trusts to add something to the experience. To watch a favorite sport, to enjoy one another's company, and, in most gatherings like this, to focus on this experience in order to take your mind off of work, family, a break-up, or similar, and focus on a single live event. Someone will win, someone will lose, and everyone watching will enjoy the time together. You are not also there to be in a hybrid Scrabble tournament that happens to be serving hot wings, beer, and Doritos. That ruins the intention of the gathering.

A lot of orchestration goes into social gatherings, but we just typically take it for granted. It is an unspoken but understood norm that you don't take a phone call during the game in the same room where everyone is watching. It is clear, often, that you need to know the basics of the game. It's also clear that, if you ridicule someone repeatedly when their team is losing, you do it within limits and within toleration. You don't show up without offering to chip in. When you get up to get a drink, you offer to grab something for others. If you hit the restroom, someone tells you what you missed. These are not trivial things, even when unsaid.

Likewise, thinking about our networks and our friendships, if we want to elevate these networks to the level of a community, we have to take responsibility for defining the norms and acting accordingly.

The challenge is that people tend to look at culture as something that is someone else's responsibility: some intangible force that is difficult to control, or simply something not worth worrying about in informal, social contexts. After all, who wants their social interactions heavily orchestrated? Yet, we argue, they already are. You just don't normally think a whole lot about the norms that are already dictated by the setting, nor do you spell them out.

Think about the country you live in or the way your family interacts when everyone gets together. The acceptable and unacceptable behaviors in each context are dictated by culture. When greeting someone, do you shake their hand? Kiss their cheeks? Bow? When gathering for a family meal, does everyone fall into specific roles, or does it shift every time? Are you able to discuss politics, or must you stick to less emotionally charged and potentially contentious topics of conversation?

Whether speaking of culture at the national, company, or a social group level, behaviors that do not fit are met with puzzled looks, at best, or complete expulsion from the group for the worst-case offenses. In this way, culture is self-reinforcing, ensuring that a group's members do things in a certain way (and don't do certain things at all). But, doing the "right" things—however defined—is only possible when powerful norms and expectations are in place.

Why, then, wouldn't you care about shaping the culture of your social world?

Culture-Focused Community

Consider the annual, weeklong desert-based event Burning Man. Even if the mere mention of the event leads to an eye roll, you cannot deny the impressive culture that has been built around it.

The Burning Man community is a celebration of art, self-expression, and self-reliance. While there is no uniform experience on the Playa (the open space on which the event takes place each year), there are ten very clear principles to adhere to. Each provides a strong understanding of the type of behavior, expression, and freedom that is accepted, but the primary principle that creates this powerful community is "leave no trace." It is the concept, universally accepted, that you remove what you bring to your campsite. Apart from that, how you conduct yourself on the Playa stays there for that unique, one-of-a-kind experience.

Making Culture Stick

When it comes to organizational culture, the concept is sometimes defined colloquially as "what employees do when no one is watching." How do people act when not necessarily being observed by others in the company? In any group—personal, professional, or otherwise—people want clearly defined "dos and don'ts," especially as they relate to ethical behavior. Perhaps not coincidentally, the OC community does not focus specifically on your professional or your personal life, instead believing that all we do is worthy of clarity around connecting.

In the quest to forge genuine connections and foster a thriving community, ethical behavior provides a cornerstone for trust and collaboration. When it comes to the way ethics are defined within the OC community, the measurement is simple: would we trust each individual in the community to be alone with our children for some (short) period of time?

Although the OC community does have shared values, this kid-related yardstick isn't necessarily about them—in fact, shared values are deliberately not part of the consideration, because they are of course not at all necessary to trust someone to watch your kids. Rather, the larger expectation/rule within this community is that one's actions should be in alignment with high behavioral standards. The kind of standards that ultimately bolster a community of people who wish to contribute to the betterment of each other and society more broadly.

To some, this may seem excessive. Most people gravitate toward those with whom they have an easy rapport, and they steer clear of people with whom they do not click or they find unpleasant. But such an approach is insufficient for cultivating a community that seeks to create the highest mutual benefit as well as a strong sense of belonging. A principled focus on expected behavior accelerates engagement within the community, while turning a blind eye to those whose actions conflict with established community values erodes the ties that bind beyond a single "bad apple."

Explicitly, in the same way that you would heavily weigh up the culture of a company you were interviewing to join or think carefully about the culture of a company you were starting, you should take a similarly hard look at the culture of the company you keep.

Elevating Group Dynamics with Expectations and Risk

When Orchestrated Connecting was first established, many intrinsically had an aversion to being reminded (even positively) that, unless they acted in a manner that elevated the OC community—with honor, follow-up, and a commitment to the community's principles—they would not be invited back to future events. There was a clear, intentional trade-off. If you understood that everyone was willing to share their connections and contacts with you (with an opt-in), as long as you would do the same for them, then you also had to understand that the code of conduct— the "mantra," so to speak—would be enforced. Specifically, if you did not act in accordance with the principles, you were out. One prominent and active OC member, the life sciences investor and philanthropist Richard Lipkin, privately told David, "It comes across as a little bit harsh."

David agreed but did nothing about it.

While the culture of any group may be defined and enforced by its leadership, because every one of us, whether gathering a group of friends, hosting the occasional dinner party, or running a business, is a walking example of the company we want to keep, we also must be clear on our boundaries. There must be thought put into our expectations around ethical behavior. But, what's more, there is risk inherent in *not* adhering to those expectations.

For example, whether at Orchestrated Connecting events or in the classroom, David and Noah do not tolerate lateness. If you are late, without a clear reason, it is a sign of disrespect. This is plainly vocalized in both contexts so that no one can claim they were unaware. It is disrespectful of our time, of others' time, and, in many of David's cases, a clear demarcation of the type of people he wants around him. Both of us also reason that, if you choose to prioritize showing up on time and participating fully in a meeting, event, or class, you will get more out of it. You are focused, prepared, and in the right space of mind. And everyone else gets more out of it as well.

We are arguing here for the importance of establishing ethics and expectations in any community. Your boundaries need not include timeliness (that's up to you), but there does need to be a mechanism for reinforcing whichever ethical norms and boundaries you put into place.

Fortunately, these already exist in our social world. They're called "reputational consequences." They drive behavior and adherence to norms, provided people understand and abide by them. We would go so far as to argue that they are essential to *any* type of community, even if it's that regular Monday Night Football potluck. No one wants to invite back the person who shows up at halftime without food or drink, asking "Who's winning?," eating everyone's food, and trampling on the atmosphere set up by those who began this shared experience.

How you communicate the expectations of a gathering or community is as important as how you define the people who are there. When you aim to elevate everyone by creating a positive, safe environment to step into, you also give permission to set ground rules. People may, for a while, seem ungrateful or hesitant to have the "negatives" positioned as part of an experience, but you can trust in the fact that most of us secretly crave rules and boundaries, within which there is freedom. Comments from OC members and Noah's students reveal exactly this.

Prioritizing Principles

Rae Richman, a long-time "Burner," founding board member of the nonprofit Burning Man Project, and member of the OC community, reflected on how she integrates the Burning Man principles into her life—both on the Playa and in her daily interactions:

> "For me, the '10 Principles' are a very valuable codification of how the Burning Man community operates and what it expects from its members. After twenty-six years, many of these core values have become so ingrained in my spirit that they naturally manifest in my personal and professional life.

> "As a professional facilitator and gatherer, I structure my events to be both organized and emergent, participatory, and co-created. In my role as a social impact advisor, my focus is on empowering myself and others toward civic responsibility. As a human, I prioritize curiosity, adventure, connection, acceptance, generosity, and accountability."

Reputational Risk

With a basic set of clearly stated and repeated behavioral expectations in place, reputational risk becomes the most important element in encouraging positive behavior. As adults building and joining social circles voluntarily, there are only so many things that can be done to reinforce norms and keep culture-eroding behavior at bay. For the majority of groups, relying on reputational risk is arguably the most powerful. While getting kicked out of a group is possible for the most egregious cultural transgressions, it is ultimately the last line of defense for OC community members who do not live the group's values. The more common reinforcement mechanism involves a member's standing and reputation in the group.

The purpose here is not to be oppressive or vindictive—note that there are not specific behavioral prescriptions in Orchestrated Connecting's "mantra" (initially shared in Chapter 2)—but to drive group member behavior toward the desired culture. In the rare cases when people do act in ways that run counter to the OC community's norms, we acknowledge that people make mistakes. The idea is to learn from the alleged misstep and correct it prior to taking action that has permanent consequences.

Reputational risk is one we live in fear of—sociologists long ago noted that "men work for wages, but they will die to preserve their status … [T]hey are usually quite unconscious of the sources of the impulses that animate them." Those "unconscious sources" are the cultural expectations of the groups in which people find themselves, and reputation is the critical incentive. It is critical because, believe it or not, your reputation is not something you actually own.

"But wait," you say. "What do you mean I don't own my reputation?" Well, you don't: reputation is shared collectively among the members of the group you find yourself in. In order for a reputation to be reinforced and for it to have consequential value, it requires others to share their opinions about you with one another. Perhaps you have moved at some point in your life. Or left one job to start another. Maybe you remember having to change schools when you were younger if your parents moved. Recall that first day in a new town, company, or school. Unless you already knew someone there, you were a blank slate. You had no reputation. You might have carried expectations with you based on your reputation in your last location, but those were only in your head. The new groups you were joining did not know anything about those expectations.

The fact that it is not something you keep with you every-where you go is the challenge of reputation. You can have one reputation among one group of people in your life and a totally different reputation among a different group. This also means rep-utation is mostly within your control. If others are required to build, maintain, and/or share your reputation, how you act influ-ences it greatly. This is why culture is such an important aspect in building community. As an individual, it is nearly impossible to maintain a bad reputation *and* be a part of a community that is fully aware of that reputation.

Of course, there are communities of assholes who congregate just as easily as purpose-driven, impact-oriented, generous human beings. But, within communities like OC, reputational risk is the lever that reinforces the focused, generative culture.

Starting Early, Staying Consistent

The initial framing of interactions is critical. By establishing the ethos (i.e., mantra) of ethical engagement upfront—*action-oriented, natural givers with whom I would be willing to leave my kids*—we empower the OC community to uphold these standards, thus ensuring that, even when lapses occur, there is a clear and just recourse to realign with our shared values. The processes by which members are introduced to the community and to each other sets the tone, fostering a culture in which ethical behavior is not only anticipated but deeply integrated into the fabric of our community.

Parents are generally taught that, unless the consequences offered to children in response to misbehavior are real, immedi-ate, and proportionate, any act of discipline will fail. Similarly, to orchestrate the desired norms and behaviors of the people in your life, you must work to create circumstances where your expectations are clear and appropriate. To that end, when people who have been "connectors" for a long time read the Orchestrated Connecting mantra, it almost always automatically clicks.

What remains unsaid in most interactions is just that: unsaid. So say it. Be clear. This intentional clarity is one of the driving forces that launched the OC community's success, and, while we recognize this "connector speak" is not for everyone, the major elements of it that are essential to purposeful interactions are.

This clarity, along with consistent reinforcement, helps instill the desired behavioral norms. The more that community members align with desired behaviors, and use the same language around them, the more likely they are to feel like they are a part of the group and to remain active contributors.

Alternatively, consider a group in which someone "ghosts"— an act that has become so common that the term, meaning completely disappearing without any communication so as to avoid people or situations rather than confront them, has become ubiquitous—after agreeing to do something. What happens if that goes unnoticed or if group members don't take steps to address and curtail it? Other group members see that, and some are likely to start thinking that they, too, don't have to follow through on commitments. The culture can unravel all too quickly.

Ultimately, the culture of a group is only as good as the worst behavior that is knowingly allowed to happen without consequence.

We believe it is now quite common to simply *not address* any challenges or problems and just walk away from issues that arise. Any community leader or even individual who sets the tone for their group, however, must confront behavior like this head on to reestablish certain norms. You must question, with curiosity, what happens from both sides and then address the people involved directly rather than avoid them. Setting cultural expectations in advance, however, will decrease the frequency with which issues arise and make it easier to address them when they do.

This brings us back to the "impact ask" from Chapter 3. If members have done their work, meaning they are clear on their needs and passions, they can step into any interaction with another community member and have the trust that their ask will be heard and acted upon.

What is most interesting to us is the fact that this isn't magical or unique to the Orchestrated Connecting network. It is quite possible to implement small measures in your daily life to increase the rate at which you establish your own trustworthiness and the speed with which you trust others. This all hinges on your ability to make your impact ask—to clearly state your purpose, lean in to help others as best you can, and be (super) clear on the type of people you want to meet. The result, should you be in the right conversation, is impassioned action.

The Difficult Work of Cultural Alignment

When Jolyne Caruso-FitzGerald reflects on the meaning of culture and looks back at the many different environments in which she worked, she notices the profound implications of a great culture versus a poor one.

A decades-long veteran of Wall Street, Jolyne was frequently the only senior woman in the room. This had a significant impact on how she conducted herself. "I had to be better prepared, more forceful without seeming aggressive, and I quickly learned not to be defensive or offended when I was challenged or dismissed," she recalls. "While I was definitely not in the boys' club, nor did I try to be, I had to develop strong emotional intelligence and adapt in order to become a successful and respected leader."

When there are more women at the table, there is an entirely different dynamic and women don't have to work so hard to be heard. At Align Impact, a female-founded advisory firm where more than half of the leadership team is female and Jolyne chairs the board, the company is led by a female CEO who surrounds herself with outstanding talent. In this boardroom, they challenge, debate, capitulate, and walk away as one team, regardless of whether their individual ideas are adopted.

Jolyne has experienced culture at its best. At its worst, she knows it invariably originates from weak leadership, creating an environment of confusion, suspicion, high turnover, and unhappiness. Wall Street is littered with stories of firms where diverse voices are stifled, leading to cultures that fail to fully develop and retain outstanding talent. While the industry has made some progress, the needle has not moved far enough.

At Barnard College, the women's college at Columbia University where she served as board chair, Jolyne learned to become a more empathetic leader, to listen intently, and to truly understand the power of respectful discourse. During her tenure, she implemented two highly sensitive and polarizing policies: to admit transgender students, and to adopt a strategy of divestment from fossil fuels for their endowment. These were difficult decisions that required twelve to eighteen months of listening sessions, outside help from experts, and rallying a board that was not unanimously in favor of either policy. Ultimately, Jolyne and her colleagues successfully aligned all stakeholders by navigating vastly different viewpoints and ensuring that everyone felt heard and considered. She believes the outcome would have likely been the same had it been an all-male board but strongly suspects the path leading to these decisions would have been very different.

Great cultures align everyone around a common goal via shared, well-understood principles. Doing so—especially when coupled with clear communication and, most importantly, trust—empowers each person to thrive by utilizing their unique skills as an individual and as part of a team.

The Five Principles of Community Culture

Orchestrated Connecting doesn't have ten principles like Burning Man. It has five, encompassing (1) diversity, (2) vulnerability, (3) curiosity, (4) generosity, and (5) gratitude. Critically, each of these requires the other four to create a cohesive and powerful culture that makes the community as purposeful and successful as it is.

Orchestrated Connecting operates by maintaining the delicate equilibrium between nurturing positive group dynamics and upholding definitive standards that guide interactions and commitments. Our members are often connected through prior interactions: professional collaborations, board memberships, social engagements, and, yes, sometimes personal relationships. Yet, familiarity is not a mandate for affinity within our community. Instead, we aspire to be a collective built on bringing out our finest selves in the spirit of embodying these principles.

While you may wish to incorporate many varied principles to your community, we believe that these five aren't just "nice to have." They are essential for any community that wishes to flourish, to empower its members, and make everyone involved better. Of course, you need not run a community in order to start applying them to your own network.

Any community that does not seek to make, for example, diversity one of its core tenets is, in our opinion, lacking. Diversity, as we will discuss in the next chapter, can come in many different flavors, but it remains a crucial element of any community.

There will be different emphases placed on particular principles depending on what your goals are, and how you create and reinforce each is of course up to you, but commitment to them is paramount. Before diving into greater depth on each principle in its own chapter, we briefly introduce them here as they relate to creating community culture.

Principle #1: Creating a Culture of Diversity

Diversity and inclusion—regrettably under attack in the United States as we write this—are too often buzzwords intended to course correct for those who seek to bolster their reputation without actually building a community, a network, or friendships with individuals from different cultures, backgrounds, or perspectives. We believe that, unless you champion diversity—because of what doing so *does* individually and collectively, not because you're "supposed" to do it—you are likely embodying the opposite of what is necessary to build a community capable of having real impact. We also believe, more generally, that refusing to see people for the content of their character is harmful to humanity as a whole.

Orchestrated Connecting was built around the concept of diversity from day one, and our events are highly choreographed. To be clear, "diversity" in our context means that every group gathering, and in fact the entire community collectively, does not have a dominant race, religion, or age range. It is also gender balanced. No room has a majority of White men or any other group in it. Purposefully.

Why create a culture with diversity? Why reinforce it? Why aim to structure the behavior of community members not just in terms of what is expected of them when interacting with each other but also in terms of how community events play out? The simple answer is trust. Meeting expectations based on past experience is a critical feature of trust, which means that *setting* expectations for how people interact within a group goes a long way toward building trust more quickly and effectively.

In a constantly growing community, there are always new people. If the community is predicated upon asking for and providing help to others, the faster that trust is established, the more effective the asks will be. As David often points out, the more diverse a roomful of people, the more opportunity there is in that room, and the more comfortable new people of all stripes will feel in making the asks to activate opportunity. When you get people to understand the strategy behind something—even something that might initially be seen as a "course correction" like DEI—they begin to see the potential for a shared and amplified vision, not one that just checks a box.

Principle #2: Creating a Culture of Vulnerability

How do you *quickly* build trust in a group so that members feel safe to ask for and provide help? It starts with the first contact that someone new has with the group. What words are used with them? How is the person treated? What is asked of them? What do they observe in others? The OC community generates vulnerability intentionally through both a culture of expressing vulnerability as well as through vulnerability-prompting exercises at its events.

Once a new member meets the group in person, culture is transmitted quickly and is reinforced frequently. And, because culture is communicated to newcomers so readily, it is essential to get both the culture and its method of transmission right. The immediate introduction into a small group in which everyone is asked to share something vulnerable about themselves serves the purpose of communicating culture and building trust quickly.

Principle #3: Creating a Culture of Curiosity

In many ways, the first two principles are nearly impossible to instill without the third. A diverse group of people is unlikely to find common ground or build trust without its members expressing genuine curiosity about their similarities and differences. And vulnerability is likely to remain confined to a small subset of group members should curiosity not be a group norm. Who wants to share something important or revealing about themselves to people who don't seem to care or want to know more?

In other words, a curiosity-free culture is one that will very quickly find itself lacking in trust. Orchestrated Connecting events are purposefully designed to generate curiosity and "build relationships at the speed of trust." Depth is added to conversations by intentionally grouping people who don't know one another, by providing advanced communication that creates a clear and safe environment, and by curating a welcoming environment from the minute a person walks into an event.

Principle #4: Creating a Culture of Generosity

Generosity comes in several forms, but our feeling is that there are two aspects that are critical for building purposeful community. First is generosity of spirit. This is the willingness to be vulnerable, to be trusting, to share of yourself and to give others the space to do so too, through curiosity and genuine regard for others' differences. Second is the kind of generosity that entails a willingness to share freely what you might have to offer. A skill, a connection, a valuable piece of information: these are the kinds of things we typically think about sharing when we talk about generosity. This is foundational in how communities support each other. One of the key features of generosity, of course, is that it is about giving without the intention of getting something in return.

Principle #5: Creating a Culture of Gratitude

Orchestrated Connecting is built upon David's "honoring the chain" rule, which serves as the cornerstone of the community's foundation and focuses on building community through a shared gratitude practice—one that lets each person see themselves in every part of a chain of connection. Sometimes, they are the "receiver": the person who substantially benefits from an introduction. Often, they are a part of the unintentional community of connections. And, sometimes, they are the "catalyst": the person who sets the chain of connections in motion, leading to a relationship that generates something substantial. If someone can see themselves as that person, they can also see themselves as the person who has *not* been thanked or recognized for spurring someone else's success.

It is because of this focus on gratitude—and many connectors' experiences of not having been thanked for a valuable introduction—that the phrase likely heard most frequently around the OC community is "honor the chain of connections" (there's a lot more on this in Chapter 10). To "honor the chain," you have to thank each individual, at least five people deep, whose connections led you to some success or opportunity.

By creating empathy for the connectors and acknowledgement for their actions from the beginning, each person subconsciously realizes that their action to honor another also contributes to honoring themselves. While all the OC community's principles contribute to a unique culture, it is perhaps the focus on gratitude—genuine not perfunctory appreciation—that truly sets it apart.

Creating Your Own Community Culture

The question remains: "How do you craft a culture for you?" Even if you have a good understanding of what culture is, putting it into action—especially in situations where people are joining voluntarily, ostensibly for social reasons—is another matter. Part of the difficulty stems from the fact that culture is viewed and learned in everyday behaviors and actions—but the real meaning of culture lies beneath the surface of those visible manifestations. According to Edgar Schein, a pioneer in the study of organizational culture, "assumptions" are the taken-for-granted beliefs about the basic underlying way the world (or a group) works. They are the ultimate drivers of behavior. Assumptions form the foundation of any culture, but, because they are taken for granted, they can be difficult to discern, even though they are so central to everything that goes on in that particular group. The everyday actions and principles you put in place send signals and messages to the members of the community about what is expected of them: those are the assumptions. It is up to you to keep that in mind and help determine what the critical assumption(s) in your community or network should be.

Armed with this knowledge, we want you to take a more conscious approach to community-building. While we lay out the critical principles for a strong community culture over the next five chapters, we invite you to think about which cultural features you would like to implement in your life. This prompt holds whether you are building your own community, joining a community, or simply looking to be more intentional in your social world. Keep in mind the specific practices you would like to implement, yes, but also pay close attention to the taken-for-granted assumptions and expectations that those practices are suggesting about the company you wish to keep.

While we believe the principles we lay out in the following chapters are essential, how you define and weigh them will create a unique mix for each community.

6

Principle #1: Diversity

———

To get real diversity of thought, you need to find the people who genuinely hold different views and invite them into the conversation.

—ADAM GRANT

Synthesizing Diversity

As a London-born, bass-playing child prodigy, Malcolm Cecil had performed regularly on weekly television appearances with the BBC's radio orchestra. He then spent time as a radar technician in the Royal Air Force before leaving to join a jazz band and ultimately co-found an early British blues band–rock group, Blues Incorporated. Though a highly respected bassist playing with musicians who would eventually end up in The Rolling Stones and Cream, a lung disease changed his professional aspirations. He moved first to South Africa, promoting mixed-race concerts during apartheid, then to San Francisco before settling in New York.

There, in an advertising agency called Mediasound Studios, he met Bob Margouleff, an American studio engineer and burgeoning synth expert, who was a friend of synthesizer pioneer Robert Moog. Margouleff had just bought himself a Moog synthesizer, which happened to be set up at the Mediasound Studios where Cecil was working as a technical engineer. The two struck up a collaboration and a deal, sharing and teaching each other what they each knew best. Reflecting on the synergy that resulted, Cecil commented:

> "Our talents complemented each other because we came from opposite sides of the spectrum. I'd be focusing on a bass line and he would go to the other end of the instrument to start with white noise. As for who came up with what, we don't know. We just found a method that made sense."

Under the name Tonto's Expanding Head Band, the two of them wrote, recorded, and released the seminal album, *Zero Time*, in 1971. *Rolling Stone* covered the album, giving it a positive review for its innovativeness, and soon Stevie Wonder—all of 21 years old but already a music industry veteran—decided to leverage his success to change his circumstances. He had been associated with the Motown record label for his entire career but sought something different.

Stevie set out for Manhattan to embark upon the next phase of his career. It would become one of the most prolific, creative, and successful runs in modern music history. *Rolling Stone* recounted the first meeting:

> "Malcolm Cecil ... 'heard a ring at the door and ... stuck [his]

head out of the window to see who it was,' Cecil recalled in 2013. Bounding down three flights of stairs, he encountered 'this Black guy in a pistachio jumpsuit who seemed to be holding our album underneath his arm.' It was Stevie Wonder."

Over the next few years, Malcolm, Bob, and Stevie would produce the albums *Music of My Mind* followed by the Grammy Award-winning *Talking Book*, *Innervisions*, and *Fulfillingness' First Finale*. All were released in a span of less than two and a half years. At one point, the trio recorded seventeen songs in a single weekend.

The technology gave Stevie the ability to control, play, and modify all the music he heard in his head, taking that symphony of sound and translating it into some of the most substantial and formative R&B records ever created. Three men from different cultures, countries, backgrounds, and areas of expertise—but all with a passion to hear sound differently—changed the soundscape of popular music. The acceptance of the differences in their expertise allowed their shared interest in creating something new and different to take center stage.

Setting the Stage

In Chapter 4, we mentioned humans' default approach to connecting with others: finding tribes of similar and typically like-minded people. In the social sciences, this ever-present phenomenon is known as "homophily"; *homo* meaning same or similar, and *phily* meaning liking or loving. It is simply easier to form relationships with people who think like us, share similar values, are from a similar background or culture, speak the same language, and have similar levels of education and income. These points of commonality are how, throughout history, we were able to quickly identify who was from the same tribe, and therefore likely to be someone who could be trusted. Identifying commonality bolstered our chance of survival when it was not assured.

However, just because it's easier to connect with people like ourselves doesn't mean it's the best way to build purposeful community, especially in an age where your aims go beyond survival.

Interacting with people who are different from you offers opportunities to challenge your principles, practice or develop your empathy, gain access to a wider range of opportunities, and redefine or reframe your needs. The value of meaningfully connecting with dissimilar others can have numerous benefits, including enhancing creativity, providing access to new perspectives, and amplifying messages. Diversity in socioeconomic status among friend groups has even been linked to upward economic mobility. However, unsurprisingly, there are geographic, social, and friendship formation biases that often limit or thwart those diverse connections from ever forming.

Fundamentally, when *we* say "diversity," we're talking about variety among our connections—welcoming others who are different from ourselves into the same spaces and places. These differences can be immediately demonstrable during an introduction or they can take time to learn about, and they can include ethnicity, family structure, socioeconomic status, age, education, geographic influences, religion, sexual orientation, physical ability, and more.

A room is not diverse if it is full only of founders. It is not diverse if it is only women or people of color. The same is true if it is only White male executives. You can't have an orchestra with only one instrument. And, in some cases, the best orchestral works involve truly non-traditional instruments—such as *The Rite of Spring* by Stravinsky, which involves a typewriter.

The challenges associated with such diversity are real, which is why setting the culture and context matter. But the benefits at the individual and collective level are undeniable, particularly when it comes to providing access to a wide breadth of unique skills, perspectives, and introductions, which is why it is the first foundational principle of the OC methodology.

In this chapter, we offer some ideas about how you should think about diversity when building community. What are some biases to watch out for, and how can you avoid them with intention? By the end of this chapter, you should not only be itching to break out of your comfort zone but have a clearer idea of how to do it, and then apply this to your own community.

Embracing Change: From Appreciation to Active Inclusion

History, time and again, has shown monumental achievements arise when diverse minds interact. From the ancient Agora of Athens to Enlightenment era coffee houses and from the Islamic Golden Age in Baghdad to modern day Silicon Valley, the history of innovation runs through places where great minds from all over could gather, share ideas, and gain access to information they would not otherwise have. The music of Stevie Wonder wouldn't exist without African American communities first bringing blues to New Orleans. There, the blues evolved into jazz, which evolved into funk and R&B and soul and all the other incredible sounds that come from the mingling of cultures to create musical innovation. Innovation goes well beyond music, of course: our comforts, our progress, our very way of life owe a lot to the interaction of people with different experiences, backgrounds, and perspectives.

Despite the fact that we owe so much to diversity, for various reasons, there's often resistance to enthusiastically embracing it. Why do we hesitate to fully immerse ourselves in this vast sea of knowledge and innovation? Perhaps it's the innate human tendency to gravitate toward the familiar, or maybe it's the remnants of age-old biases that still linger in the shadows of our society and many others. Our innate social drive pushes us to connect but then isolates us into homogenized groups.

While we have deep respect for any group that brings together those for whom their diverse background alienates them from what is the "norm" in some way, we want to encourage you to think of those groups as diverse only in comparison to the homogeneity of a group made up of a given society's majority demographic. Neither type of group is actually diverse. Each creates an echo chamber environment that not only neglects the innovative cross-pollination of ideas, but also creates powerful norms of conformity that lead to more isolation.

In today's digital age, we're paradoxically both more connected and more isolated. While we have the world at our fingertips, many (often aided by social media algorithms) choose to remain in those echo chambers, listening only to voices that mirror their own beliefs and experiences. Breaking out of these confines and truly embracing diversity is not just beneficial, it's essential. It enriches our worldview, fosters innovation, and helps us tackle global challenges more effectively. The alternative—a collection of increasingly isolated, internally homogenous tribes—is a grim picture. A world like that would be incredibly antagonistic. Currently, it appears that we are regressing. We are aiming to avoid that fate.

A move beyond mere appreciation of diversity to active inclusion is essential to propel society forward, and it starts with our own communities. Not just celebrating the differences but weaving them into the very fabric of our daily lives. Asking for the diversity that you seek. For, in the fusion of diverse threads, we craft a tapestry that's not only vibrant and beautiful but also resilient and forward looking. "Craft" is the critical word here: simply putting diverse people together and hoping for some kind of alchemistic magic to make it all work is likely a failure path. Structures and systems need to be in place to avoid the difficulties of difference and instead ensure that the benefits of diversity become reality. Systems also need to be in place to mitigate discomfort or risk that could be associated with inclusion. If, for example, women are made to feel welcome but that trust is taken advantage of by a guy in the group, diversity isn't going to last long (recall the story of Drake from Chapter 2).

In every Orchestrated Connecting event David hosts, he works to "craft" a more inclusive environment. Most importantly, he builds diversity into his events by purposefully creating a balance of gender and a mix of ages and occupations, while keeping a strong core value of focusing on the content of every person who attends. Then, within the first few minutes of his events, people are put into an intimate group setting where no group is of one gender and all have varied make-ups. Everyone must answer questions that seek to reveal their common humanity, rather than highlighting their differences.

The curiosity to embrace this core "content of character" approach creates a structure where everyone feels heard and seen, and therefore no one feels or experiences the sense of alienation or difference that you might feel when stepping into an unknown environment. There is, instead, (social) attraction.

This journey starts locally. Note, too, that integration—not full "assimilation"—is key. Assimilation means losing the distinctiveness and variety that makes diverse groups interesting and dynamic.

Leading with Diversity-Oriented Action

Kojo Annan is a strong example of the creation of a community—a business—that celebrates diversity in action.

Kojo, an OC community member of Nigerian and Ghanaian heritage, grew up surrounded by an international crowd, as a result of his father's work as secretary-general of the United Nations. He is an independent spirit with a multicultural community that spans Africa, Europe, and North America.

Kojo's purpose is to change the global perspective on African culture. He believes that, once the world sees the African continent for its people, its innovation, and its beauty, it will change the image we have from the 1990s of starving children in Ethiopia. His need is to change the African narrative because his belief is that the current worldview about Africa is false. His vision is for all African nations and peoples to define their own legacy. His work begins from the starting point of this purpose.

A serial entrepreneur and investor, Kojo co-founded Made in Africa, a company he still chairs, in 2018. It is a technology-driven apparel trading company focused on sustainable manufacturing. The company helps develop high-growth early-stage brands to become market leaders and it manages export supply chains for global brands that are moving their manufacturing base to Africa. The company, under Kojo's leadership, focuses 50 percent of its investments on the continent with the remainder of investment made in brands in other parts of the world that can be backward-integrated into an African supply chain. Made in Africa is committed to maintaining 50 percent of its board seats being held by women, and comprises mainly people of African descent.

African culture represents incredible diversity of language, heritage, and history, and, while we may generalize or group all as "African," the truth is Kojo brings together a myriad of cultures and groups toward a common, greater cause.

In 2020, Kojo further demonstrated his commitment to his values and to elevating African culture. Based on its rich diversity of people, its architecture, and its innovation potential, Kojo made the choice to move his family to Ethiopia, putting his energy, money, and time in support of his value system. As he has matured in his business, he has worked to step back and have others come to him, rather than heading out to meet the world and make his mark. His approach is about depth, and seeking those who share his purpose.

By rebranding people's perspective through food, fashion, art, sports, film, music, and an immersion in the diverse landscape throughout the continent, Kojo maintains a belief that people will come together to celebrate differences in ways similar to the way that dominant "cultural forces" in politics, economics, and media do so today. But, in this case, with a prominent African voice.

Conducting the Orchestra: Connecting with Diversity

For many groups, celebrating diversity unfortunately means something along the lines of "course correcting and adding a small, insignificant number of different people and pretending they have changed the whole of it." This is especially true in the Western business environment, where most have a few minority group "tokens" surrounded by homogeneity.

Of course, you cannot course correct your social biases via window dressing. You must do so by intentionally engaging meaningfully with people different from you. A "token" is still a token. To make that course correction, you're going to have to embrace a broader community than the comfortable one of similar-looking and like-minded people you most easily fall into. And, in so doing, clearly define your values and needs, bringing in people whose vulnerability and passions—whose humanity—add to your own. It does you little service to align yourself with individuals who don't awaken your passions, embrace your values, and challenge your goals.

Let's put it more plainly. You can't just go out and add people who are diverse to a group that has an intention or a purpose. If you run a book club and you bring in new members who add to the diversity of your group, but they don't speak your language or don't want to read the books, you didn't achieve much. This is why crafting diversity has to be accomplished by developing a value system with core values, and then "shaking the tree," so to speak, to bring in individuals who share your values. As the quote that started this chapter suggests, you have to invite those diverse individuals into the conversation.

Building a purposeful community therefore means instilling this value of real diversity from the beginning. Your shared purpose, based on clearly defined values and a rigorous defense of the community's boundaries, is what will bring and keep you together. Intentionally open doors to seek out and bring in those who do not "look" like you but "sound" similar to you *in response to that purpose*—even or especially if they don't always "sound" like you in terms of other perspectives and opinions. Remember that we often look superficially, selecting for shared background, when we should look deeper and select for "content of character."

To do so, you will have to be curious and willing to question or even abandon your assumptions about an "other." That is why, though diversity may be the first principle, it is not the only one. The others make engaging with diversity possible.

Diversity in the OC Community

> As I built my business, even after years of being a successful NFL player and then winning the Super Bowl, I continued to notice that, while people loved the fame, they wanted to wait to focus for our meeting until my business partner, Jonathan [Ohliger], would arrive. Everyone wanted to be around me, but they wanted to hear from him. We are equal partners; the only difference, [as] he points out, is he looks more like most of the rooms we walk into, not me.
>
> **—NAJEE GOODE, EAGLES SUPER BOWL LII CHAMPION AND OC COMMUNITY MEMBER**

The reality in the OC community is that you are likely going to find yourself stepping into a room where White men are often in the minority (the irony of the two of us writing this book is not lost on us), where women commonly outnumber men, and where there is typically a plurality of races and ethnicities present. What's striking is that this composition goes largely unnoticed until highlighted. The absence of any immediate labeling or feelings of tokenism reveals the group's norm.

When diversity is made foundational, it—like many of the other principles and practices within the OC community—simply becomes part of the community fabric. There is no pretense made about it: it just is. On the other hand, it is predominantly in contexts where power and hierarchical dynamics already exist that diversity for the sake of diversity is so noticeable. This is not to say that the existing societal power structures are simply left at the door in communities where diversity is baked in from the beginning, but that is where the rigorous introductory process, consistent reinforcement of community values and culture, and regular rituals come in.

A lack of diversity is the result of someone's or some group's not having been intentional about emphasizing the crucial role played by diversity in elevating collections of people, be they a small group of friends or whole societies. And, whatever you may feel about it, the primary point for us is that you need to actively seek to achieve it. You need to ask for it and not accept that it is not possible to create a group that is gender balanced. That it is impossible to meet the "right people" who happen to be BIPOC. Or that you just can't find the right candidate for the job who isn't like all the other candidates you've hired before. You won't always achieve it, but we all can certainly do a lot more by making it intentional.

Foundational Diversity

Consider, as a compelling example, the astronomically successful Broadway musical *Hamilton.*

Lin-Manuel Miranda has helped redefine America's history, taking the founding history of America and turning important pieces of it back into a story of immigration and diversity. He did this by excerpting an integral part of modern American society (spoken word/hip-hop) and smartly combining it with history that has been all too frequently overlooked in historical accounts. Black and Brown individuals are very much a part of that history, and a more complete telling serves not only to inspire marginalized individuals and communities but also proves the central role that diversity played in our history. Black and Brown individuals also dominated the cast, even if the historical figure they were playing may have been neither.

Personally for both of us, from the musical knowledge deep in each of our lives, it is clear that, without bringing African populations to the US, the creativity of jazz, rock and roll, Motown, soul, R&B, hip-hop, and even country music would not exist as we know it. We wouldn't have the visual and auditory representation of how divergent but equally "American" cultures could combine to create the best music written over the last century.

Despite the fact that, when combined, they make up the *majority* of the world's population, women, racial and ethnic minorities, and people with social, economic, physical, or mental challenges still struggle to find places of belonging in many areas of public, political, and social life. For example, female members of our community have changed their names to be more gender neutral, or altered their family name to conform to the culture they live in because they were tired of being passed over without being given a chance over and over again.

A major reason why correcting these societal ills has proven so difficult is that people in power believe they give up their power by doing so. It has been our experience in the OC community that they do not, yet people in most contexts with power continue to cling to this fear. While changing power structures in any one generation is a tall order, building purposeful communities that mirror what society will become increases the odds that those structures will eventually evolve. Small changes at the individual or local level quickly add up to much more widespread societal changes.

Putting Diversity into Practice

Having your existing perspective repeatedly played back to you does not do much for your growth, nor for learning. It does even less to help society.

And, look, we get it. Most people, even those who are open to the idea of more diversity in their social life or professional lives, tend to fall short when it comes to having true diversity in their network. We're not saying you need to drastically change your closest set of friends, but we would ask you to consider this: how many of the people with shared passions, the ones whose time you value beyond just circumstance or upbringing, are actually just like you in terms of age, gender, sexual orientation, etc.? At the writing of this book, the fact is a minority of Americans have college degrees, roughly 40 percent of the country is non-White, and 51 percent of the country is female, to say nothing of the ideological, occupational, and socioeconomic diversity present. Presumably, that means you have many options as far as finding people a bit different from yourself to bring new perspectives into your life. This "access" to variety extends beyond people currently in the majority demographic.

However you approach it, diversity needs to be embraced fully. Our society depends on it. Just Google "*Fortune* 500 companies founded by immigrants." Hold on—back up a step because, actually, Google's existence stems from the minds of immigrants (as does roughly 45 percent of the *Fortune* 500). In fact, roughly one in six inventors in the US between 1990 and 2016 was an immigrant who came to America as an adult, and they have had an outsized impact, accounting for roughly a quarter of the patents and economic value generated from those patents. Immigrant innovators also spur other innovators more than native-born innovators do. The benefits of diversity don't come exclusively from immigrants, but they provide a striking example.

What we would venture now to say, and this is David's stance in speaking at conferences in particular, is that, unless we become a champion of diversity, working actively to be inclusive and open, we are instead working to maintain the status quo. Such inaction is to the detriment of everyone, whether in minority or majority communities.

Identify Your Biases and Room for Growth

Our guess is that, while many of you can identify the music of the heavy metal band Metallica, many of you reading this would never ask Alexa to play the band's music. Yet, if we were to play the band Apocalyptica's version of Metallica's song "The Unforgiven," you might recognize the melody played by the band's four Finnish cello players. At the very least, you would note the gorgeous, lyrical, and dynamic music. The song is one of Metallica's biggest hits, but their metal version doesn't accentuate the same level of lyricism that you can hear in Apocalyptica's unique instrumentation. The two groups share the same musical language and interpret it differently—by having both in comparison they are each richer to listen to.

You might be inclined to think that you've already got the Orchestrated Connecting diversity principle covered in your life.

Maybe you've traveled abroad and made friends from other countries, you speak a second language, or you belong to a community, in person or online, where the majority of people in attendance are from underrepresented groups.

You might also belong to the opposite camp. You may not see the need to embrace this principle because it feels contrived, unnecessary, or, on some level, threatening. For people in this camp, the move toward diversity seems rushed, forced, and at the expense of their current cultural practices.

Regardless of the camp that you see yourself in, we would invite you to consider this question: "What is holding you back from reaching out of your comfort tribe?"

The fear of not belonging is one of the many things that re-entrenches us in tribes: we reach out to those whom we think are experiencing the same discomfort, those whose worldview makes us feel like we're right. It's called "echo"—you're likely familiar with the concept of an "echo chamber"—and, in groups of similar people, it serves to reinforce our existing views and those of the others closest and most similar to us. Finding ways to create a sense of belonging *in a group of people who don't share your perspective* is critical.

Take homosexuality, for example. The data shows that, historically, the further back you go, the more challenging it was to identify as gay, but that, the more society integrates, the more accepting cities and communities become overall. This is not to say there aren't still inherent challenges and legal battles faced by many; just that it is better than it was ten years ago, and beyond. Imagine a reality where diversity is embraced but so is your unique value system, where you don't feel threatened by this move toward embracing difference. That's the goal here.

To achieve this goal, you need to be aware of your biases. And remember, before you get annoyed, we all have biases on all kinds of different topics. A "bias" is simply a tendency or inclination based on your past or experience, though we often refer to them when they negatively influence our judgment. To overcome those biases, you have to honestly recognize them. To get a sense of whether this is the case, ask yourself if you have any negative feelings, including feelings of guilt or pity, that come up when you think of:

- people whose sexual preferences or behaviors are different from yours (this includes the entire spectrum, from polyamory to chastity until marriage)
- people who practice their religion on a daily basis (think about all religious beliefs)
- people who don't practice any religion at all
- people who fill out their ballots differently to the way you do
- people who have a lot of money or who came from money
- people who don't have any money or who came from poverty
- people who were born with disabilities
- people who served in the military

A "yes" to any of these questions might suggest a bias just as much as a negative reaction to a person of a different race or gender. We would challenge you to stretch your mind and think about how your purpose and values could still be shared by people who are different from you in these ways.

This leaves us with the question of how to broaden your perspective and become more inclusive of those who are different from you.

There are specific tactics and goals to find others with shared values who are different from you. Individually, you can seek out diversity by pushing yourself outside your comfort zone, embracing new people as original and fascinating. However, we recognize it is simply more comfortable and "normal" to walk up to groups that look like you. So, how do you break out of this habit?

Let's start by asking some questions to determine what kind of environment you are in or the background you come from:

1. If you are a college graduate, how many friends do you have who did not graduate from college? And vice versa?

2. Of the friends with whom you spend time on a monthly basis, what percentage have a different cultural background than you?

3. When was the last time you had a conversation with someone whose perspective on a topic that was important to you was significantly different from your own perspective? How do you handle such conversations when you realize how different those perspectives are?

4. Do you deliberately avoid befriending people—or even having conversations with people—you suspect hold different political beliefs from you?

Our Call to Action

It begins with new practices. Change your routines. Attend different group's meetings. Invite others to join yours. Start with small interactions with someone who very likely isn't going to share your perspective on something.

What we have found, as it is part of the Orchestrated Connecting model, is that by sharing your values and your passions, and simultaneously asking for more diversity in your network, people can help you identify, or engage from, a more diverse lens. It is the combination of "asking for it" while also asking for the diversity to align with your values. It takes intentionality and an understanding that there are many perspectives outside one's own.

There are several approaches to simply asking for more diversity. Once you define the areas, ways, or opportunities in which you can add it, be clear on the need beyond diversity itself. For Orchestrated Connecting, we know that diversity is key to larger, more powerful networks, and greater outcomes in connection.

If you need more examples, and here are a few among many, you could:

- encourage more hiring practices that reflect the outside world
- add more equal representation—not just a symbolic diversity officer—to leadership
- ask individuals to attend events to show they are allies of those of differing backgrounds to gain understanding of another perspective
- reach out to a co-worker or colleague with genuine curiosity about their experiences
- attend multicultural or multi-faith events
- invite someone with differing beliefs to a neutral place, like joining for a walk or coffee, to get to know them better, even if it's only one time to start

7

Principle #2: Vulnerability

Why Vulnerability?

Opening Up to Build Community

If the core of community lies in shared vulnerability and understanding, Natasha Müller is this essence in human form. A philanthropist, impact investor, and beacon for mental health awareness, Natasha understood intuitively that vulnerability, understanding, and the type of community that each can help build are not merely about connecting individuals, they are fundamentally about weaving together stories, passions, and purpose.

Natasha's advocacy for mental health was deeply personal. The early loss of her father due to mental illness ignited a spark within her. She speaks bravely about his death, sharing her vulnerability in a way that helps others embrace their own challenges more directly. While incredibly connected and well loved, like many leaders she felt

105

alone, and wanted to support others who felt similarly. In turn, she wanted to be supported in achieving her impassioned goals in the often fragmented and isolated field of mental wellness. Recognizing the necessity of the power of community to address this issue, she reached out to Rachel Gerrol, co-founder of the NEXUS community. Rachel helped Natasha envision a mental health collective, drawing inspiration from NEXUS's model, with Natasha taking up a pivotal leadership role.

While mental health might seem like an obvious foundation for community, the irony lies in the innate isolating effect of mental health struggles. Recognizing this disconnect and the need to first be willing to share her own connection to the issue, Natasha aimed to bridge the gap with her collective. Opening herself and her experience with her father up for others to see, Natasha's initiative began with connections in her immediate network, establishing a group of people who mirrored her values and were all active in the same space, though mostly independently. From that foundation of vulnerability, hers has evolved into a formidable network of global mental health advocates. Lady Gaga—no stranger to vulnerability, having created her community of "Little Monsters" in part by opening up about her own struggles with mental health— is a member of the network through her Born This Way Foundation, as are leading corporate magnates, and other high-profile individuals, this community is redefining advocacy. Natasha named the community "Kokoro," a Japanese word that refers to the indivisibility of heart, spirit, and mind. It is redefining mental health advocacy.

Kokoro is also responsible for convening the Future Mental Health Collective, a network of mental health investors and philanthropists. The Collective, like Kokoro, emphasizes the universal nature of mental health struggles, debunking the illusion that affluence negates mental health challenges. Despite societal, political, and medical barriers, this group works tirelessly to highlight the significance of mental health, emphasizing its parallel importance to physical well-being.

Initiatives within this community are always collaborative. A poignant example was the rapid response during and after the 2023 Türkiye (Turkey)–Syria earthquake. Leveraging community resources, they swiftly facilitated the deployment of Arabic-speaking therapists to care for trauma victims in Turkey by combining two different philanthropists' networks of resources.

The foundation of Natasha's community is authenticity and humility. Egos are checked at the door, and members are focused solely on eradicating the stigmas attached to mental health. One of the defining principles of the community, which Natasha is quick to mention when asked, is clarity in membership. Inspired by David's approach to community, she emphasized that the success of a purpose-driven group isn't about inclusivity for the sake of inclusivity. Instead, it's about carefully curating members who prioritize collective needs over personal desires—much like how David and Rachel approach their respective networks.

Natasha summarizes her intentions this way:

"Each of our groups was tackling a major issue in mental health independently. We were operating in silos both topically and geographically, while ironically all focused on the isolating stigma associated with even talking about mental wellness, illness, or fortitude. I had to build a group where the intentions were to lean in and to learn and grow together, not just share our goals and get everyone to align purely and perfectly to ours."

Kokoro is one of the most substantial existing communities of wealth holders and mental health activists tackling mental health directly, with people funding philanthropic projects and seeding or building new start-ups. The community effectively pools each individual's drive so that the collective can focus on larger issues and support each other in that journey.

But it began—and begins—with Natasha's vulnerability. Without a willingness to share her personal connection to mental health struggles and the profound loss of her father due to those struggles, Natasha's group would be a community of one. Instead, her opening up prompted a desire to work on the issues in a more public setting. The members of Natasha's community are sincerely vulnerable, revealing the deeply personal "why" behind their active support of those in mental crises. By sharing with one another and with the broader mental health community in this way, they create a beautiful bond with each interaction.

Strength Through Vulnerability

Building trust is not just the fundamental component of any relationship; it is especially crucial when dealing with people who are different from you. It follows that the chapter after our discussion of diversity is one about vulnerability, helping you understand why it works and how to do it appropriately. It is a cornerstone of the Orchestrated Connecting methodology, and it has become an integral part of Noah's teaching practices. Deep connection pays off just as much in the classroom as it does in the boardroom, city hall, the team huddle, and the dinner party.

This chapter digs deep into the psychology of vulnerability and human connection, providing examples of when and why it is so effective. We also highlight how *not* to be vulnerable.

The Basis of Trust

Why do you trust the people closest to you? Is it because you are required to do so because of familial ties? Does your history and experience with friends mean that you simply continue to trust them without question? Has a previous collaboration or prior interactions with someone led you to believe that person will continue to act in your best interest? Do you judge these situations and relationships based on past involvement, gut instinct, or both?

Chances are each of these is true, depending on the person in question. Academics have identified two main variants of trust: cognition based and affect based. "Cognition-based trust" is a function of prior evidence or experience with someone setting the expectation of future reliability, while "affect-based trust" is based on genuine care or concern—and the hope that it is or will be reciprocated. For our purposes, the specific definition matters less than its role as the foundation of relationships.

Trust fills the gap between complete knowledge of someone else and complete ignorance of that person. If you know absolutely everything about someone and the context in which you encounter them, there is no need for trust, and, if you know absolutely nothing about someone, you have no grounds on which to establish trust. Therefore, based on some degree of information about someone else and your understanding of the context in which you are meeting them, trust is an (incompletely) informed way of hoping that person will look out for you and your interests. You can see why it is such an important feature of community-building.

How does vulnerability fit in? Vulnerability is such an important aspect of trust that most social science definitions of "trust" include in them a willingness to be vulnerable, in hopes of that vulnerability being rewarded and/or returned. The less information you have about the other person, the greater the need for vulnerability on their behalf (and yours, as well), which signals their willingness to step into the potential relationship, even if it means they may get burned as a result.

More generally, the first gesture of vulnerability has the potential to set two people off on a path of building a stronger relationship (see Figure 1). That initial *vulnerability* from one person, when offered at the appropriate level and in the right circumstances, sends a signal of *trust* to the other. It has the ability to spark *curiosity* in the person who was on the receiving end of the vulnerability, and it invites some degree of vulnerability in return. With increased recognition of each other's humanity—what is vulnerability, after all, but a revealing of your humanity?—there is going to be greater *empathy* between the two people. That is, there will be a better, more genuine understanding of where someone is coming from, what some of their values might be, and why they may respond in a particular way to a set of circumstances.

This is extremely subtle, and there is no one recipe. But, instead of oversharing, or just asking people deeply personal questions they are not ready to answer, we suggest that approaching others with curiosity and empathy is central to finding a path to meaningful connections and relationships.

If both people in this interaction have developed some empathy for each other, each will feel greater *safety* and a stronger connection (i.e., a sense of *belonging*) to the other, which, in turn, again increases *trust*. And off you go in the development of a deeper relationship. It is, ideally, a virtuous cycle.

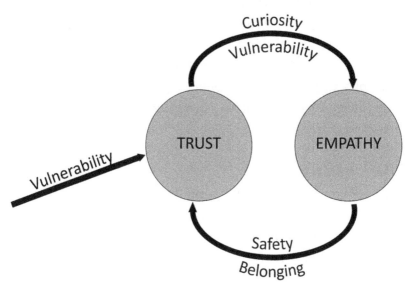

Figure 1. The "Connection Flywheel":
How Relationships Develop

Noah developed this Connection Flywheel model after having spent a year interviewing members of the OC community and using vulnerability exercises in his classroom. It captures the development of any relationship, whether personal, professional, or familial. You have to begin with vulnerability to build initial trust, and, from that trust and subsequent vulnerability, the cycle of empathy and trust creates safety and belonging.

Building beyond one-to-one relationships, when two or more individuals share a bond of trust, that trust can be extended and enhanced with others because of the trustworthiness signaled to others by that bond. This is not just lived experience talking: researchers have demonstrated that greater "social connectedness"—more friends and acquaintances in common—is likely to enhance perceptions of trustworthiness. When structured properly, that trust can be encouraged among those who have not yet built it with a purposeful introduction, staking one's reputational value on the potential for that new relationship to flourish.

For nearly a decade, that has been one of the foundational principles of Orchestrated Connecting. Not only can trust be built but transferred and deepened through encouraging vulnerability and shared passions.

To Share or Not to Share?

OK, you get it: vulnerability is key to building trust. But what exactly do we mean by vulnerability? What gets shared? In reality, it can be anything that reveals some aspect of your human experience or fallibility. But it goes beyond that: it must be genuine. That is, it must be something personal and unique to you, but that also connects you to common experiences or feelings of others. It is not particularly vulnerable to say "My parents are getting older," as everyone's are. To instead say, "I'm struggling to deal with the fact that my parents are starting to forget so much that I worry if they can take care of themselves" is much more specific and connected to your lived experience. It is therefore more genuinely vulnerable.

It is unfortunately all too easy to share something that seemingly reveals a failure or moment of humanity but is either made up or inauthentic. Sharing that a grandparent recently passed away when you had no real relationship with that grandparent as a means of trying to engender sympathy is manipulation, not vulnerability. Or sharing every bad thing that has happened to you that day—like what your worst airplane seat neighbor did to you that one time—is also not vulnerability. Vulnerability has boundaries.

If the idea of being truly vulnerable fills you with anxiety or dread, that's normal. But it doesn't make it any less necessary. In order to build your own community or further connect with others around this principle of vulnerability, you must first explore your own behaviors (and, likely, reservations) around this concept.

Holding Yourself Back

You have probably experienced a situation—personal or professional—where you have guarded yourself, your feelings, or your perspective; a situation where you have self-regulated, opting not to respond to someone's comment or action with your desired response but with something you deemed safer or more socially acceptable. Maybe you chose not to open up about a topic where you could truly connect with another person. Perhaps it was to save face or prevent embarrassment on your part. Maybe there was a part of you that felt that if you reciprocated vulnerability, you would lose some perceived supremacy you had gained in that interaction.

Say a co-worker opens up about her weight-loss struggles, relationship issues, mental health challenges, or the difficulties of being a working parent. Instead of disclosing that you, too, had similar struggles in the past, or may even be experiencing them right now, you keep quiet, choosing to simply listen because being in the listener or advisor role is more comfortable. To be clear, we're not suggesting this is always the wrong thing to do, but, when you do it, you are in effect masking your authentic self. You are guarding against deeper connection. Most people tend not to realize that this kind of regulation, especially when repeated over time, comes with a cost.

When we routinely self-regulate—a common behavior among motivated, ambitious, socially aware individuals—our willpower to continue to do so diminishes. With it, so too does our energy. Over time, in addition to this ego depletion, routine guarding of ourselves and our thoughts not only reduces our energy, it leaves us feeling unknown. Isolated. Lonely. The exact opposite of the goal of community. We become so confined in our own heads that we don't believe we will ever find someone to truly know us. The truth is that we have gotten further and further away from finding ourselves, and it wasn't the fact we didn't meet the right other people; it's that we didn't open ourselves up to do so. In contrast, by being vulnerable, we allow others to do the same, and we find strength together.

This idea extends to situations where you may perceive a wrong or injustice being done. Not speaking up similarly comes at the cost, not just to your willpower and energy, but also to the community or group in which the wrongdoing takes place.Sometimes, speaking up when we feel we ought to comes with a genuine risk to our job or our social standing. But, by not responding, we are allowing the negative patterns, which might be unsafe or brutal, to continue to affect each person individually.

While we are not suggesting that the only course of action is to always call out bad behavior directly, we do believe that being vocal about why you choose to not associate or engage with someone does, crucially, call out that behavior. In a strong enough community or movement, such as #MeToo, the willingness to be vulnerable can cause real positive change in entrenched and pathological power structures.

Think about when choosing to be closed off and not vulnerable has been helpful to you, or if you are even aware of or able to track an outcome in which being closed off has actually gotten you ahead. Can you think of an instance in which the opposite has happened? Where you have felt compelled to share and be vulnerable, and it has brought you closer to your purpose, your values, your community?

To quote the musical *Hamilton*, "If you stand for nothing, what will you fall for?"

Tiny Lights of Connection... or Floodlights

A few of us have the opposite tendency. Rather than a reluctance to be vulnerable, we tend to overshare. This leads to awkwardness and actually creates barriers to connection.

Author, podcaster, and patron saint of vulnerability Brené Brown describes connection via vulnerability as illuminating tiny lights of connection: little "a ha" revelations that draw people closer to each other. However, she also notes that oversharing—basically vomiting your personal secrets and shortcomings all over someone else—is more akin to flood lighting. Oversharing is overwhelming, self-serving, and goes against the spirit of connecting via vulnerability. A critical first step in the connection process is, therefore, *appropriate* vulnerability. It is a disclosure that something may be difficult, that everything is not perfect, or that, simply, you are human. And it is doing so in the right context, as appropriateness is of course context dependent.

If you personally can't relate to having overshared, you have, at the very least, likely been on the receiving end. You encounter someone—could be a stranger, a co-worker, or even a friend of a friend—and you strike up a conversation that starts off comfortably in standard small-talk territory. Next thing you know, they have launched into a lengthy list of grievances or personal information, revealing far too much. Maybe they are describing something deeply personal about their marriage or their partner, something that you are certain the person being discussed would not be happy to have revealed. Or perhaps they are sharing the intimate details of a recent medical issue that feels a little graphic. You can probably think of an example of this kind of uncomfortable oversharing relatively easily because it tends to stand out.

Odds are that the place in which the story was shared or the person sharing it wasn't "right." Let's say the person sharing the medical information was seated next to you on a flight and you'd never met him before. You might feel a little uncomfortable—it depends on the level of detail provided—but you likely would chalk it up to oversharing, maybe share a much less personal story in return, and then get back to your earbuds and podcast. But, if that airplane seatmate was a colleague with a desk next to yours, it would feel far more repellant.

What these examples reveal is that a combination of personal preferences, physical setting, and relational proximity determines what level of sharing is appropriate. While a complete stranger can of course completely put you off with a far-too-intimate detail, sometimes someone with whom you have no friends in common can feel like a safe person to share important personal issues with, and often these friendly strangers can be receptive and even helpful. The perceived safety you feel is because your reputation faces little risk when you are vulnerable with that total stranger: they have no one you know with whom to share the potentially juicy details.

It tends to be the "in-between" relationships—the "weak ties" you know and may have a friend or two in common with, but don't know well—with whom you face the greatest perceived risk from sharing. While a close friend or family member has a lot of connections in common with you, the depth of trust built means you're likely safe revealing an intimate detail. But, the weak tie is the most dangerous: close enough to know a few of the people you know but not close enough to have earned the trust. And guess which kind of ties you are likely to encounter when entering a new community.

The question is, then, how to create the right context for vulnerability to be appropriate and safe?

Connecting in the Classroom

As mentioned, Noah has borrowed quite a bit from David's Orchestrated Connecting methodology to quickly build community and create a culture in his classes. While it begins with his syllabi, which point out that class will be in-person and students are expected to be on time, the stage is really set once students show up on the first day.

After a brief introduction to whichever course it is, Noah reminds students how learning, especially learning about yourself and others, happens: by nudging yourself outside your comfort zone. Only then can new habits and patterns develop and fresh insights come about.

Using this push to encourage students to step out of their comfort zones, Noah then suggests that the class build community and step into this "learning zone" at the same time. He breaks students up into random groups of four or five, gives them a vulnerability-inducing question like those Sarah was asked in Chapter 1, and sends them off to breakout rooms for fifteen minutes to meet one another. What is important is that Noah has set the stage for his students to be open to sharing something vulnerable and to do so within a group of diverse students who do not know each other.

Noah was anxious the first time he tried this with executive groups. Would these senior leaders be willing to do something as exposing as this? And what happens if people just give surface-level answers, and no one really gets much from it?

Fortunately, after over four years of doing this introductory exercise, such difficulties have almost never come to pass. In fact, the connection created right off the bat sets the culture for the rest of the course or program: a desire to connect, a willingness to be vulnerable, and a commitment to themselves and the other students. After that, it almost doesn't matter what the course content is. If the students have bought into the culture of connection, openness, and trust, the rest tends to flow quite easily.

But what about those groups of students in which the first person to share is guarded, or not comfortable sharing something that feels too exposing? Certainly, this is a reasonable reaction for someone who feels like they are putting themselves at risk. In groups like this, one of two things tends to happen. First, if the second person to share is similarly guarded, a culture of minimal trust is established, and the rest of the group members will tend to refrain from making themselves vulnerable. It is a perfectly understandable response: "Why should I trust others in the group if they so clearly do not trust me?"

The other possible response is a second group member who does not follow the more guarded lead of the first. By showing a willingness to be vulnerable, even when the first person in the group did not, this second person is trying to reset the culture in the group to one that is more trusting. The rest of the group members usually follow suit. And the initial responder—the one who did not feel safe enough to share—often will chime in at the end with something that shows that they, too, now feel greater trust.

Fostering Connection

Because being vulnerable is an art more than it is a science, the Orchestrated Connecting methodology uses questions specifically aimed at generating reciprocal vulnerability early on in each of its meetings. These questions go beyond a simple self-introduction about where you're from and what you do for a living. There is even a book filled with exactly the kinds of questions that prompt people to be more vulnerable: *The Book of Questions* by Gregory Stock.

Having witnessed the speed with which people form genuine bonds as a result of these kinds of questions, Noah uses them in the introductory exercises mentioned above, as opposed to standard icebreaker questions, which many people tend not to like very much anyway.

"But wait," you might be thinking, "Won't someone—especially in a professional context—take advantage of whatever they learn about me?" Well, they might, and this concern is not all that surprising. As humans, we pay much more attention to the downside potential of a given situation than the potential for a comparable (or possibly even greater) upside. However, in overestimating the possibility that our vulnerability will be used against us, we overlook the downsides of *not* being vulnerable, of not establishing genuine trust and connection, and of not building empathy in our relationships.

Manipulating relational closeness by prompting vulnerability may sound like a strange social experiment to you. And, as luck would have it, it was one. In 1997, psychologists and spouses Arthur and Elaine Aron (along with additional co-authors) published a study in which they tried to generate feelings of closeness between pairs of strangers in a lab setting. Pairs were set up in various ways across the multiple experiments: some pairs were matched for agreement or disagreement on important attitudes. Some pairs were primed to expect that they were going to like their partner, while others received no such expectation. And some were explicitly told that the goal of the experiment was to like their partner while others had that information withheld. All pairs were either given a set of increasingly personal, vulnerability-inducing questions or standard small talk/surface-level questions.

The different ways in which pairs were formed or prepped did not make much difference. Instead, the big differences came from the types of questions pairs asked and answered. Pairs that asked vulnerability-inducing questions had significantly stronger feelings of closeness after the experiment than did those that asked the surface-level questions.

Crucially, for the closeness-generating pairs, the questions started off relatively general and grew increasingly more personal. The experiment began with questions like "When did you last sing to yourself? To someone else?" before moving on to something like "If a crystal ball could tell you the truth about yourself, your life, the future, or anything else, what would you want to know?" And then, finally, one of the last questions might have been "Your house, containing everything you own, catches fire. After saving your loved ones and pets, you have time to safely make a final dash to save any one item. What would it be? Why?"

If these sound like the kinds of questions Sarah had to answer at her first Orchestrated Connecting event, it's because they are exactly the kinds of questions David uses.

The results of the Arons' study were so compelling that, nearly twenty years after it was published, the *New York Times* published an article titled "To Fall in Love with Anyone, Do This." In it, the author recounts her own personal experiment with the full list of thirty-six questions published in the original study, and how it led her to beginning to fall in love with the person with whom she went through the questions.

The Risks and Rewards of Vulnerability

It is not unreasonable to worry that we might be engaging in our own social experiments with vulnerability. In addition to concerns about being taken advantage of, you might be wondering if we are simply instrumentalizing vulnerability, using it "artificially" to give people a sense of comfort and trust that may not be real. Even though the methodology clearly works, that concern is legitimate.

However, it has been our experience that many people—most, even—*want* to be vulnerable. They want to trust. They want real connection with others. The above *New York Times* article received eight million views in its first month online and was covered by newspapers and websites around the world. It even featured in the *New York Times*'s own compendium of the fifty best articles that had appeared online since the paper started offering digital subscriptions. Clearly, vulnerability not only works for generating closeness, but it is of genuine interest.

Yet, because of our increasingly polarized and winner-take-most world, the risks of vulnerability lead us to protect ourselves. Whether at an Orchestrated Connecting event or in one of Noah's classes, we quickly create the space—setting the right context to provide sufficient trust and safety—to allow people to get back in touch with that desire for genuine connection. The upshot is that, once vulnerability and the safety that goes along with it is established as a group norm, it has far-reaching benefits for everyone involved. Ironically, individual vulnerability decreases group-level vulnerability (i.e., the likelihood that the group falls apart or is taken advantage of).

This is apparent when you attend an Orchestrated Connecting event, or when you happen to meet a small group of members at another conference. There is a difference between this group's members and others because there is not only mutual trust and vulnerability but also a natural curiosity about other people and a willingness to step away from one's more guarded nature with new people. There is trust in the curation of the individuals who are in the community.

It is through vulnerability that you come to know yourself better too. It is difficult to know where you sit until you hear (or read) where you stand—and then have that played back to you, in the form of a response, deeper engagement, and reciprocated vulnerability. Connecting back to our music metaphor, gauging your wavelength involves vocalizing your frequency and intently listening for the echoes—be they the hush of understanding or the crescendo of shared aspirations.

Revealing something of yourself and having that genuinely and positively acknowledged has recently been labeled as "being seen"—being understood for who you are and where you are, psychologically or emotionally. Going back to the Connection Flywheel depicted in Figure 1, being seen creates a sense of belonging, which increases feelings of being part of a community and something greater than yourself. Once again, we have a virtuous cycle.

Intentionality in Openness

Intentional vulnerability is key. To reveal your inner realm, you must invite others in. If you want to show off your physique, you need to wear the right clothes to do so. Likewise, showcasing your wit or, conversely, delving into the depths of a personal loss and ongoing healing requires giving voice to those emotions. All the while, you are likely to be a little uncertain of what responses you might get in return.

The thin line separating vulnerability from perceived self-absorption lies in crafting opportunities for mutual sharing. It's not merely about ensuring your voice is heard but equally about ushering in a chorus of shared or similar experiences. To forge genuine connection and foster community, there must be both an understanding of yourself and a committing of yourself. And there must be space for you to allow others to do the same.

This is why, in addition to accelerating the "getting to know each other" process that any group of people will go through, vulnerability provides an opportunity for self-reflection that plays back into the Orchestrated Connecting idea of purposely asking for what you really need.

Seek and You Shall Receive

One intentional practice in Orchestrated Connecting is informally called "fishing with vulnerability." Not to be confused with "faux vulnerability," which cynically tries to mimic genuine connection without real openness, "fishing with vulnerability" instead refers to the windows during which real connection can be established during a first encounter.

When meeting someone for the first time, you will often find a few minutes of opportunity during which the door for sharing your purpose is open. This works unless you're talking to a self-interested individual who meets people to talk about themselves, and then feels the meeting went well because of it. In those instances, well, you're out of luck.

Based on dozens of conversations with OC members and others, David considers that different profiles, or personality types, tend to approach these first five minutes of conversation slightly differently, but with roughly the same notion of having a short window during which they can find their route in.

- Strategic interviewers often believe they have five minutes to ask the right question.
- Extroverts often believe they have five minutes to tell the right story.
- Introverts often believe they have five minutes to listen well and help the other be heard.

Each perspective holds merit, yet there's a subtle nuance to consider. You have the power to change the trajectory when conversing with someone absorbed in their own narrative. The key lies in gently steering them away from their familiar patterns. It's not about merely being an audience to their monologue. Instead, it's about engaging with intentionality and purpose, finding a way to reinvent the dynamics of every interaction.

Break down your own patterns of conversation and see how that can break down others' as well.

Genuineness and Generosity

Here are our suggestions for building vulnerability into any conversation—with the goal of building community in mind.

Step 1: Initiate with Openness

Begin with five minutes of genuine openness. Aim to share at least three personal insights that are intimate but not overly so. Create an atmosphere where the other person feels safe to lower their guard and be authentic. This genuine beginning sets the tone for the entire conversation, preventing biases, habits, or superficiality. What you are ultimately looking to avoid, when possible, is the "LinkedIn introduction": all the things someone can learn about you from a quick glance at your LinkedIn profile. That has its time and place, but it tells others little of who you really are, highlighting things—where you work or went to college—that lend themselves to comparison and status differentiation rather than connection. On the other hand, if you initiate with vulnerability, you will be more likely to maintain that authenticity throughout.

Too often in conversation, the real substance only surfaces toward the end. Maybe it's a request someone hesitated to make or a revelation that could've changed the entire course of the dialogue. To truly connect, it's imperative to shake things up and put others a bit on their toes. Authenticity, vulnerability, and breaking your own habits are crucial for this.

Initiating with such openness and prompting someone to reciprocate accomplishes this primary step.

Step 2: Listen Actively

Listen actively and delve deeper into their words. Listen to actually hear, not to just respond when there's an opening. For instance, if they bring up a recent holiday, don't just ask about the location; question how they carried the vacation's positive vibes into their daily life or what was the most surprising thing they encountered during (or reflecting upon) the trip. Engage in their narrative, then subtly redirect the conversation in the direction you intended it to go.

A strong start is just the beginning. If you're unable to respond constructively to what someone reveals, it's a missed opportunity. Consider the analogy of jumpstarting a car: initiating is essential, but, if you keep your foot on the brake, you're not going anywhere. It's less about your speaking and more about letting the other person experience a novel way of interacting, where they feel truly heard. And, in case you need another incentive to do this, research shows that people who ask more questions—especially follow-ups that indicate paying close attention—are more liked than those who ask fewer in conversation.

Step 3: Share Goals

Time to get their consent to share your core passions and objectives. Don't reserve your true intention for the end. If you've set the tone right and shown you're attentive, this is your golden moment, your true five minutes. Starting with vulnerability, uncovering shared goals, and then expressing hopes of mutual interests is the way forward. The objective isn't to have them remember every detail but to leave a lasting impression with a few poignant points.

Remember, if you directly state your wants, they may not resonate. However, by conveying your passions and the drive to magnify them—namely, your genuine need—you establish connections that foster community. This is the challenging part.

Step 4: Offer Assistance

Conclude by genuinely offering assistance. This shouldn't be a mere formality or contingent on their response to your earlier points but a sincere gesture of generosity. And then, of course, follow through.

Our Call to Action

Don't be afraid of vulnerability. As with much of the framework we are detailing in this book, making the implicit explicit—or simply stepping into what may feel culturally or contextually uncomfortable—tends to be welcomed and rewarded. Being vulnerable is no different. You will be pleasantly surprised by the kind of response people have to sharing something personal and humanizing in the context of getting to know them, working with them, or just briefly crossing paths.

By allowing yourself to be vulnerable, and by creating the space and a receptive context for others' vulnerability, you can connect with the members of your community on a deeper level.

♭ ♭ ♭

Remember the nightmare that opened our book? Where you step out onto a stage and can't remember how to play piano? Vulnerability is not being OK with the fact that you hit the wrong notes. It's the sense that, as you continue to play and hit the wrong notes, you internalize the music, the emotions, and the "flow," continuing to make it your own. This practice of vulnerability isn't about throwing up or out all of your emotions, but, rather, the delicate balance of what you do, in the face of being in a situation where you can't figure out exactly what to play. Embrace your own insecurities, understand your own needs, and find the right balance.

8

Principle #3:
Connecting with Curiosity

Our brains can't hold the energies of judgment and
curiosity at the same time.

—VALIA GLYTSIS

Wanting to Know More, Without Judgment

One of Noah's mentors is a genuine innovator in the education space, especially when it comes to developing current and future leaders, and his approach is predicated on
curiosity about self and others. Gianpiero Petrieglieri is a
Sicilian-born doctor who made the somewhat unusual
move from medicine into leadership development. Very
quickly, he and a couple of like-minded friends realized
that there were not many spaces in which leaders and
aspiring leaders could find themselves that were conducive

129

to confronting themselves, their past, and their biases yet still feel "safe."

Armed with his background in psychiatry and a desire to humanize leadership, GP (as he is known) developed in-class and "in the field" activities, centered around small groups. The activities are intended to create challenging situations and dynamics—for example, a difficult ropes course exercise where only one person in a group has access to the rules and goals and must do their best to communicate them to the others. These activities, the group debriefs that follow, and the individual reflection prompted by it all pushes people to be curious about their mindsets, reactions, and innate tendencies, as well as those of the others in their group.

For participants, it is not easy work. You're not often prodded to figure out why, for example, someone who initially came across as particularly friendly quickly turned on you as soon as frustration with an inability to accomplish an ostensibly reasonable task set in. Nor are you typically prompted to consider why *you* reacted the way you did when facing similar frustration. However, the experiences invite you to acknowledge your assumptions and, for the truly curious, to genuinely inquire how and why those assumptions came to exist in the first place—and what those assumptions do to the people you work with.

As Noah has served as both a faculty member and a small group observer/consultant in some of GP's programs, he has seen firsthand the power of these exercises and experiences, particularly in terms of provoking exactly the kind of curiosity we believe should be embedded in any community. It starts with curiosity about yourself but extends—quickly and intentionally—to the experience of others around you. People leave the programs genuinely transformed.

GP likes to close his programs by stating: "You don't need to be perfect. You need to be awake." "Awake," in our interpretation, means curious about what's going on in and around you.

Why Curiosity? And What about That Cat?

You can't write about curiosity and not talk about why it killed the cat. This old adage is a code, and, to many, a warning to "mind your own business." But, as with vulnerability, our premise is that, without curiosity, you close yourself off to opportunity with all people except those who are quite similar to you. Without a mindset of openness to other viewpoints, you are unlikely to find any kind of middle ground from which to move forward with whomever holds that other viewpoint.

We're not just spouting "*kumbaya*" nonsense here: research shows that curiosity is a significant driver of building tight-knit relationships. That is because curiosity not only leads to better responses and reactions to the kinds of self-disclosures that we have already discussed and that are more common among curious people, but also because curious people tend to be more responsive to subtleties shared by others. These kinds of behaviors make relationship formation—*especially* when differences exist between two people—easier, faster, and more enjoyable.

Many people in positions of power often purposefully strike chords that make you—or, crucially, others—feel or seem different. And, when you succumb or become numb to the lack of curiosity that enables such othering to take place, you cede control to someone else, often those leaders.

But the minute we start to ask questions or take in other viewpoints, we begin to see that things are rarely as black and white as they are painted. And that, by not being curious, we may have given away too much. The "product" we desire only solves an immediate want. The "politician" we voted for said a lot of things and didn't do them. The corporation that promises to hire more women does… but at lower wages.

It is easy to feel too often exhausted or too busy to be curious. Yet, curiosity actually can fuel us, give us the energy we need, and motivate us to develop further. Our belief is the more we orchestrate our lives and build purposeful community, the greater our ability will be to transform our society from one that is easily divided because of apathy into one of abundance, fueled by genuine curiosity.

One of David's dad's favorite shirts from the company Mental Floss has printed on it: "Apathy… I can take it or leave it." That apathy is the antithesis of curiosity. Curiosity is an active mindset that combines empathy and inquisitiveness without judgment but with a desire to understand more than you currently do. It turns "others" into your community.

The curious cat, as the story goes, is relentless. It continues to play with a wild animal until that animal's true (aggressive) nature rears up. It's likely why we say cats have nine lives: they need them. But, want to know the true irony of this phrase? Most people aren't curious enough to simply Google it, which would reveal that there is a second half to the quote that we typically miss: "but satisfaction brings it back." This part of the quote implies that the challenges and the risk the cat took are ultimately worth it. The true risk, then, is in *not* leading with a curious mindset in the first place. Effective, purposeful communities work to tap into all the curiosity that children have.

Seeing Things for the First Time

Noah and David both have young children and find parenting an ever-rewarding experience—observing, studying, teaching, and nurturing minds that see the world completely differently than they do. It's a fascinating experiment, fraught with the need to find some kind of balance between how much you affect your kids and how much to let them be just who they are. Faced with such a challenge, what can you do? You pay attention and you do your best (which never feels good enough). Then you realize over and over again that they've been studying you—not just when you're parenting but in every other moment as well.

Kids haven't yet formed their worldview, and so much of what they encounter is new to them, putting them in a position where they must be curious. They are constantly studying the world and trying to put things in place. Their innate curiosity comes from a need to make sense of what often isn't sensible, or at least isn't immediately so. This means that they engage with the world in a much more open-minded way—unlike the way most of us do, which is driven by confirmation bias. Yes, we all, to varying degrees, seek out and latch onto things that reinforce our existing set of beliefs.

However you approach life, a great deal of how you respond to things comes down to whether you choose to be curious about what's in front of you—taking an abundance mindset of "I have the opportunity to learn something new and expand myself"—or you are resolved to slotting it into what you are already convinced of. Until we realize this, we have only a small degree of control when it comes down to our reactions to new or different things.

This concept of approaching life with wonder is sometimes called "*Shoshin*," which comes from Zen Buddhism and means "beginner's mind."

Taking a look at those who thrive—the world is filled with examples of leaders, creatives, builders, and innovative people of all types—we generally see people who have a childlike, innate curiosity for life. They believe things can be different from the current status quo, and take others along for the ride. Though tribal tendencies still exist, there is also increasing celebration of those who share distinctive perspectives and create new ways to look at the world.

These innovators take what we expect, and they give it a voice that is distinctly their own. Go back to pop music and spend time listening to cover songs of your favorite song. You can often quickly distinguish between artists who are very good technically and those who excel at taking something you know and reinterpreting it into something you know *plus* more. It is no different among non-musicians or any other type of creator, inventor, or builder: if there's nothing new under the sun, the innovators see something through a unique lens and take our known or existing world and reframe it in a unique and compelling way.

Optimally Distinct

Do you know who Karl Martin Sandberg (aka Max Martin) is? Unless you're a pop music superfan, odds are reasonably high that you don't. But—and here's where we again encourage you to be curious—know that, if you have listened to the radio or a streaming service in the last quarter century and hummed any of those tunes in the shower, you certainly are familiar with his work.

Max's influence on pop culture is remarkable. He is, as of October 2024, second only to Paul McCartney in terms of number of *Billboard* number-one singles written. When you listen to his hits, especially as a trained musician (David) or someone who studies what makes hits stand out (Noah), you understand the brilliance of how he structures his songs. He varies the basic structure and harmonies that our ears ache for, yet he maintains enough of a familiar sound to still notch twenty-five Grammy nominations and five Grammy Awards. You hear this all as familiar, but also new at the same time. It's that balance of novelty—provoking the listeners' curiosity—and familiarity, which gets you humming along as if you've known it your whole life (even though you haven't), that makes him so successful. The concept is called "optimal distinctiveness."

By way of illustration, the structure of most popular music follows a general pattern that looks like this:

> Intro
> Verse > Chorus > Verse > Chorus
> Bridge > Chorus
> Outro

There's not much variation. Comedian Hannibal Burress said it best in one of his stand-up specials, *My Name is Hannibal*:

> "Gangsta rappers always talking about shooting people and killing, but they still stick with song structure, like, perfectly ... [*imitating*] 'I would talk about killing more, but that was the 16th bar and I gotta go to the chorus now. I want to be a *marketable* murderer.'"

Everyone, even Max Martin, sticks to the structure, because it's familiar, which makes it even more fascinating when people break that mold, surprising you with something unexpected.

You can typically rattle exceptions to the standard structure off the top of your head, because they're so rare and so distinct: think Queen's "Bohemian Rhapsody," Lady Gaga's "Shallow," the Beatles' "A Day in the Life," and even Prince's "Purple Rain" mixes things up a bit. Tweaking the structure, even just a little, invites curiosity and increases memorability. The same holds in interpersonal interaction.

Curiosity in Conversation

Think about how curiosity comes into play in your conversations with other people, especially people you are meeting for the first time. When we first wrote this chapter, we estimated, based on experience (i.e., not scientific analysis), that only around 30 percent of the conversations that we have entail the other person asking anything at all meaningful about us—as opposed to the other person simply talking or us simply asking questions about the other person.

It turns out that we were not far off. Researching the structure and content of conversations, we found observational studies suggesting that 30 to 40 percent of conversation in "relaxed social settings," even among those who already know each other, is about revealing personal thoughts, opinions, and relationships. That is, communicating whatever is going on inside the speaker's mind. This is compared to very small percentages of conversation spent asking or giving advice.

The other primary topic? Gossip, which serves the purpose of reputational positioning, defining social boundaries, and enforcing social norms. In other words, people are busy signaling that they're on your team and that they have important things to share, but not that they want to know much about you.

While not the same as only 30 percent of *all* conversations including so much as an incoming question, the data still suggests that most interpersonal social interaction is about sharing our own thoughts and perspectives. Perhaps it's because the reward centers of the brain—think dopamine, which we will discuss in the Chapter 9 in relation to generosity—light up when we are talking about ourselves but not when we are talking about or judging the traits of others. It appears that we might be hardwired to be self-centered in conversation.

This is where breaking free of the standard structure comes into play. Cue curiosity.

Just like songs that break the traditional structure, you likely can recall particularly memorable conversations (especially first conversations) that you've had, because they, too, are so rare and so distinct. While finding common ground stems first and foremost from whether you choose to be vulnerable, so much of it comes down to moving past standard pleasantries and engaging with your conversation partner(s) with curiosity. Curious people ask questions, and they similarly thrive when asked a question that sends a signal that they were heard, or that we are about to have a real, optimally distinct conversation.

When it comes to connecting, particularly in the context of a burgeoning community, we think this is the point: having a conversation about something meaningful that brings purpose, depth, and possibly an outcome from that connection. Unfortunately, we—and scientific research—find this to be rare, despite its being the point of "putting yourself out there." The same researchers who found that pleasure centers respond to talking about yourself also found that the research subjects were willing to forego (admittedly small) payments to answer questions about themselves. This was especially the case when they thought they were sharing that information with another person, as opposed to answering the questions privately! People *love* to talk about themselves.

So, what do song structure and curiosity have to do with our hypothesized 30 percent? They all speak to the fact that a bit of differentiation sparks curiosity in the audience, whether that's someone streaming a track or engaging in a conversation. If the majority of our interactions follow a structure, in the same way that the majority of songs are written with the same structure, then those who break the mold are likely to stand out. And, once something changes our perspective—a slightly tweaked structure, a poignant question—it can start to feel like it always belonged. When this happens with relationships, you build depth to the point that it feels like the speaker of that initial curiosity-laden question has always been part of your life, even though they haven't.

Perhaps it's worth asking a new question. Maybe, early in your next conversation with someone you've just met, rather than running through your usual small talk routine, you ask "What are you most excited about these days?" And then, watch how the other person responds—likely with some initial surprise and then some appreciation for the different prompt—but also watch how you respond. Are you genuinely curious?

Life-Changing Events

In interviewing dozens of OC community members for this book to learn more about "how they tick" and their thoughts on connecting and community, we were particularly surprised by one common experience. Nearly all of the roughly fifty people we initially spoke to mentioned a life event, often including a physical or emotional trauma, that was overcome (fully or partly) relatively early on in their lives.

First, it is worth having a definition of "trauma," so that everyone understands we're not just throwing the term around to cover anything deemed as difficult or negative. According to Dr. Paul Conti, a Stanford- and Harvard Medical School-trained psychiatrist and trauma expert, trauma is "something that overwhelms our coping skills and leaves us [as well as our behaviors and brain functioning] different as we move forward." While we are not experts on determining what qualifies as a traumatic experience, to the people we spoke with, their experiences generally seemed to rise to this level.

Importantly, this was not something we asked about, nor was it something we were seeking. Rather, early traumatic experiences were often offered when Noah asked how they came to understand the value of being generous with their time and advice to others, often strangers (a topic we will cover in Chapter 9). Their acknowledgment and processing of some traumatic event—few shared specific details, for understandable reasons—seemed to have led them to become more generous, a "giver."

We do not wish to glorify traumatic experiences in any way; they remain horrible experiences that you have hopefully avoided, and we recognize that experiencing trauma will certainly not always lead to such pro-social outcomes for many people, nor is it a prerequisite for building community. That said, it was notable how often it came up. In the population we interviewed, perhaps the genuine connectivity and generosity they demonstrate throughout their lives is one way for them to work through or overcome such trauma, which consequently creates greater empathy for others.

There is research that suggests that curiosity may have a positive effect on flourishing and well-being among teenagers who experienced childhood emotional abuse. This is due in large part to the way that curiosity—specifically, the kind of curiosity that relates to searching for novel experiences and situations—dampened the negative effect of the abuse on self-compassion, which is the trait that was connected to the teens' flourishing.

Perhaps our discovery of the connection between curiosity, a willingness to be vulnerable (and creating space for others to be too), and well-being makes sense. Though the people we spoke with didn't necessarily share the intimate details of their trauma, their continued effort to work through it not only instilled their own curiosity about what others were going through but also invited curiosity from others in their interactions.

While our sample remains relatively small, it is large enough to indicate a trend, especially as those interviewed were somewhat randomly selected from among the OC community.

A question for you, then, is have you, to some degree or another, been informed by challenging circumstances that caused you to grow and evolve from them into supporting others?

Trauma can come in many forms—childhood illness, surgery, death in the family, incidents of bullying, or other types of adversity—but what is clear is that, when faced with a need to repair or to fill a void that takes months or years, the people we spoke with overcame their trauma by making it a part of them. To be clear, this occurrence is, to be clear, something that changes your worldview, often challenging it, and that forces you to re-evaluate how you lead your life and how you can move forward.

Ultimately, this dramatic change of perspective is the main difference between those "raging against the dying of the light" and/or "living lives of quiet desperation" (see Chapter 3) and those living lives of purpose. In the former two cases, what haunts us can be unresolved because we choose to ignore it, or not face it.

It can eat us up inside while we create an external world to mask or exclude that from our psyche. We believe that we must move from being guarded to being vulnerable, to being truly resilient, in order to achieve this.

This is true for both Noah and David personally as well. It is part of the journey we each went through—and are certainly still on—to build the resiliency to balance parenting, creativity, ambitions, and other responsibilities that came out of us realizing we needed to build a new, broader skill set to thrive.

Unwillingness to Be a Victim

There is a difference between someone who is a survivor and someone who is actively working to help others avoid or recover quickly from their trauma. The individuals we have found who take steps to help others regularly are innately curious about others. Most people find themselves "surprised" that they are opening up so quickly to someone they just met. Whether you are the person opening up or the person inviting that vulnerability in, the combination of trauma and curiosity—which seems to be related to the trauma—is a phenomenal study in resilience, kindness, vulnerability, and generosity. More than anything else, it appears to be a catalyst for building relationship trust both quickly and purposefully.

Among the people who shared with us their experience with trauma and overcoming it, we typically heard an unwillingness amongst them to be a victim, or to act as a martyr. Unfortunately, we all have lived with, dated, or worked with people who have a martyr complex. And, while the foundations of many religions lay in self-sacrifice, the difference is between self-sacrifice for the greater good and for an individual want or desire.

Normalizing the Abnormal

There are, of course, many ways to respond to traumatic experiences. We're not at all qualified to tell you how to do it. Instead, we wish to point out what we heard from the members of the OC community who we interviewed, and to share it as a means of providing insight into how some people effectively connect.

What is striking about the people with whom we spoke—and whom David knows from their involvement in Orchestrated Connecting—is their resilience. They actively work to engage others and do everything in their power to help them avoid a traumatic experience. Or, at the very least, to recover quickly from it. Their leaning in is often shocking to those whom they don't know, but their poise and ability to make other people comfortable builds trust, and from that, relationships.

The challenge is that they tend to normalize what others would think to be an abnormal or triggering experience, leaving some shocked when they speak of their trauma with a sense of normalcy. But their intention is to lead by example, and to take active steps to support others. By working through their challenges, resolving them as much as possible, they bounce back more quickly and work to help others.

The ways in which we allow circumstances to define us creates our "way of being" in the world. That's one of the reasons we've chosen to dig into trauma here, specifically in the chapter on curiosity. What we have found to be most curious (pun intended) about those who face their traumas is that they tend to be the most curious about themselves *and* about others. Their perspectives and curiosity about life are utilized to better inform and recolor their own. The more they are curious about other perspectives, the more they, like you, can actually develop and work to form more purposeful communities.

This principle of curiosity is core to Orchestrated Connecting, which is why simply just improving yourself and identifying your purpose is not enough. You must also work to understand and challenge those around you, tracking your growth alongside theirs. And, to do that, you must be vulnerable enough to let others in and then curious enough to spark their vulnerability in return.

The Resilient

If you have read or studied the American psychologist Abraham Maslow's paper "A Theory of Human Motivation," in which he spells out the five needs that make up his famous hierarchy, you might be surprised to find that some believe there is actually a sixth need. This need is the full evolution of self, according to David's friend and OC community member, Jenny Santi, or "self-transcendence." And, for us, this new perspective leads to a focus on the character trait of resilience.

Jenny is a psychotherapist and artist whose career started in philanthropy. At a relatively young age, she was the head of philanthropy services at the bank UBS, advising ultra-high-net-worth clients on their charitable activities. She subsequently published a book, *The Giving Way to Happiness*, chronicling her journey. She was also the first OC community member interviewed at the very beginning of this book project.

What Jenny taught David years ago is that people often view actualization as the final step—but some people view self-transcendence as an even further evolution. As she explains in a chapter in her book titled "From Trauma to Triumph," the transformation of someone from traumatized into a thriving giver speaks specifically to how one builds and develops resilience.

Resilience is a strength borne of curiosity when put in the context of connection. It is a practice that allows you to bounce back from adversity and difficulty. Having the confidence in yourself to recover from adversity and thrive is inherently part of the growth that you undertake while addressing your needs within Maslow's hierarchy. Fundamentally, these encompass physiological, safety, love and belonging, esteem needs—all of which lead to the top need of Maslow's original hierarchy: self-actualization.

"Positive psychology," introduced around the turn of the twenty-first century by psychologist Martin Seligman, is key to this. While self-actualization is the process of realizing your full potential through intense personal growth, self-transcendence creates a connection to something greater than yourself—note the connection to our definition of purpose. An abundance mindset, the purposeful practice of gratitude and curiosity, and a positive mentality are what can set you on the path to self-transcendence and help you build the skills you need to continue to grow past self-actualization.

This is what makes the strongest of us resilient, because our perspective isn't only about our needs, our goals, or our challenges—it is also about the greater good. And it is why we argue that the inclusion of self-transcendence, stemming from curiosity, enables us to build what can truly create lasting change in our world: purposeful community.

What Killed Curiosity?

Our lack of curiosity about other perspectives, and the lack of work to find common ground, is harming our society. This isn't about finding the right answer, though; it's about finding others who want to learn, share, and grow together in their perspectives.

As Noah and David raise their respective children, they try to keep that sense of innocence, that belief in possibility, alive as long as they can until their children step into a world where not everyone gets what they want. They try to teach them to be civil about disagreements and perceived unfairness. To be honest and just. And they celebrate their curiosity and smile at a worldview they hope they maintain as much of as possible as their children grow up.

When you meet curious people, you realize that they somehow found ways to maintain this childlike quality while growing up. Whether it is something you've held onto since childhood, or you feel may have died, you can work to build (or rebuild) and maintain curiosity as part of a mentality that doesn't have to accept the ways things "must be." People with curiosity thrive, and they are also those parents who find ways to love life even with the challenges of parenting one or more small children. They make it work and find a balance because they operate with the same curious mindset they are seeking to instill. Later in life, that same curiosity may even help slow the aging process. Just in case you needed another motivation to be more curious.

Curiosity killed the cat because it assumed the risks weren't worth it. A purposeful mindset changes this, and, if you remain vigilantly curious, you won't need nine lives, because you will have one that allows you to maximize your potential and that of those around you, too.

Our Call to Action

Follow your natural inclination to want to know more. Put bluntly: be curious. Pause initial judgment for as much time—and as often—as you can.

The most important steps you can take are as follows:

- In conversation, start with curiosity about the person you're talking to; specifically, about their experience.

- If they ask you a question, be willing to be vulnerable, but don't make it about you—make it about both of you.
- Be open to following a conversation where it will go, without an agenda, and try to keep in mind that most people in the world will see things differently than you do.
- And then dig deep down and try to keep perspective on why someone isn't as curious as you are and how you can bring that out in them.

Curiosity may have killed the cat... but satisfaction brought it back.

9

Principle #4: Generosity

———————

The wise man ... enjoys the giving more than the recipient enjoys the receiving ... None but the wise man knows how to return a favor. Even a fool can return it in proportion to his knowledge and his power; his fault would be a lack of knowledge rather than a lack of will or desire.

—SENECA, *LETTERS FROM A STOIC*

Small Blocks of Generosity

At the beginning of the very first COVID-19 lockdown, Noah was living in France with his wife and two young children. He had no other family around, and he and his wife were housebound with the kids. It was... not ideal. Given his interest in connection, a genuine desire to feel like he was contributing something to the world during the pandemic, and a need for some activity to keep him from going crazy, Noah decided to embrace a spirit of giving and curiosity, rather than be dragged down by confinement.

As a professor, he was used to hosting "Office Hours": a block of time every week during which students could come to his office to discuss topics of their choosing. While this is intended to help explain material and concepts from whichever course he is teaching at that moment, it often becomes a discussion about students' career aspirations and fears, or a similarly personal topic. Based on his having held these for years, Noah decided to take advantage of the fact that the world was now smaller—everyone was on Zoom or Teams—and offer "open to anyone" Office Hours.

A brief LinkedIn post explained the idea and included a link to a Google Sheet spreadsheet. Anyone who came across the post and wanted to discuss something related to an area in which Noah felt he could offer positive input or guidance was welcomed to sign up. He put twenty-four fifteen-minute slots on the Google Sheet, published the post, and figured that, if his sister was the only one who signed up (because she felt sorry for him), he would learn his lesson and move on.

Within three hours, all twenty-four slots had been filled. Noah posted twenty-four more slots for the following weeks, and those, too, filled in another three hours.

Within a couple of weeks, Noah's initial post had been viewed over 30,000 times; he had something like 3,500 connections and followers on LinkedIn at the time.

Following that initial "launch," Noah holds open Office Hours on about thirty Fridays per year, blocking an hour or so roughly every other week and welcoming anyone who wants to chat to sign up for a 15-minute block (now run through Calendly). All Noah asks for from anyone interested in participating is a sentence or two explaining what they would like to talk about. This short description of what the person signing up wants to discuss aids in redirecting anyone for whom Noah is unlikely to be helpful. It also increases the commitment from the person signing up. There have been precious few no-shows in over four years of hosting these. He has now had over 200 conversations with people through the Office Hours, nearly half of which are with people he had never met in person nor had any direct connection.

The Office Hours have led to conversations with people in over thirty countries and at all career stages—from an undergraduate interested in knowing more about pursuing a PhD to someone who worked at the Pentagon and wanted to chat about what he should do in his retirement. When Noah sees it on his calendar on a given day, the first reaction is often an "Oh man… why am I doing this again?" At the end of the hour of speaking to people, however, he is energized and inspired. All because of people's willingness to share their own experience and the vulnerability of asking for help.

Noah started the Office Hours with no expectation of getting anything in return for them. They were—and continue to be—an opportunity to connect, to provide some help, and to learn about others. Yet, each conversation typically ends with genuine gratitude from whomever he is speaking with, and an offer of anything they could do to help Noah. He has never taken anyone up on it.

Furthermore, the Office Hours idea is what led to Noah meeting David. Noah's former student, Jamil, upon hearing and reading about what Noah was doing with the Office Hours, recognized the similarity in values with David, prompting the introduction.

Noah's initial curiosity about others, and desire to provide what felt like a small bit of help, played a role in the creation of this book.

Why Generosity?

Generosity goes hand in hand with both vulnerability and curiosity. You must be giving of yourself if you are to truly be vulnerable, just as you must be generous with others in granting them the time and space to share their own vulnerability. And curiosity requires a generosity of interpretation: if you are going to dig deeper into someone's story, past, or passions, it is necessary to do so without judgment. You have to take in what they are saying with openness, particularly if they are sharing a different perspective than that which you hold.

Once this type of generosity has been established in your community (or your team or organization), sharing personally revealing stories and feelings becomes substantially easier. So, too, does asking for help. Like vulnerability and curiosity, generosity is contagious: modeling giving behavior encourages it in others.

As far as we are concerned, a relationship is not give and take. It is give and give. Whether we're talking about time, attention, vulnerability, or more tangible items, offering something of yours because you want or expect something in return is not a particularly helpful way to go about things, at least not in the long run. It's one of the reasons many people are uncomfortable with networking: feeling like you are being introduced to someone simply because they want something feels awkward at best, transactional and instrumental at worst. But if everyone in a group defaults to giving, there is a much smaller need for taking or being transactional.

In these more transactional situations, don't expect to be truly thanked. However, in situations where genuine generosity is offered and real gratitude is returned, there is an increase in reputational value as trust is further built. The interaction serves as a positive example of the giver's reputational value, whether they asked for an increase in their reputational value or not! True generosity is not about satisfying your own ego, pocketbook, or anything but the spirit in which something can truly be given. No strings attached. The increase in reputational value is just the icing on the cake.

Reputational Value

Reputational value is the ultimate arbiter of how you are described to others, by others, without your being there. The more universal or consistent you are in your actions related to generosity, the more well defined you are not just with your reputation but also the value attached to it.

There are many things you can buy, but you cannot change your reputation based on how much you spend; you can only change it by what you do. You can be an amazing lawyer or doctor and still be an asshole. You can be a visionary founder but also a creepy psychopath. You can be many things, but, if you are valued for who you are and what you do, it is because people can see consistency in you and your actions. The more you live by your values, the more people come to realize that they are getting a consistent and authentic "you," and the more likely they are to share with others the value in action you've brought to them. That authenticity in action becomes a manifestation of your reputational value as you accomplish time and time again what you say you will do for different people in different groups.

Having high reputational value means there is widespread understanding that the combination of your words and actions are positive overall. Despite your flaws or challenges, you are judged based on the successful carrying out of your intentions.

Generalized Reciprocity

Generosity, like so much else within a community, requires the establishment and persistence of trust because, in a diverse community, there is rarely a circumstance where the person being helped is able to reciprocate the exact gesture to the person who helped them. Plus, this kind of direct give–get is transactional, which belies the point of generosity in the first place. To that end, yet another critical aspect of the OC community design is setting the tone such that people can feel comfortable either advocating for what they need or advocating for others' needs without the other party being concerned that they are being taken advantage of.

We spoke briefly in Chapter 4 about the power of reciprocity, explicitly a "norm of reciprocity" that encourages the returning of favors to the people who have done favors for us. At the individual level (individualized reciprocity), this can be viewed as instrumental or used just for personal gain: "I'm only helping you so that I can eventually ask for something in return." But the generalized version of this—"I'm going to help you because I know that our community will ultimately help those in it who ask for it" (generalized reciprocity)—is an incredibly powerful force.

This kind of generalized reciprocity is the idea behind the Reciprocity Ring exercise popularized by Adam Grant, and further elaborated on by the idea's co-creator, Wayne Baker, in his book *All You Have to Do Is Ask*. While Grant and Baker both describe the exercise in detail, the idea is simple: create a small group of roughly ten people, typically within a company (though Noah and others do the exercise in educational settings), and encourage everyone to come up with a detailed, specific ask for something that would be meaningfully helpful to them. Sound familiar? Within each group, odds are high that someone will be able to help, either directly or by making an introduction to someone else who can. The exercise encourages everyone to do so with specific details of when and how they can help.

Critically, while the person who helps on any given request is unlikely to have the favor returned directly, at least one person in each group is likely to step up for another member's request. This is because we have found it extremely rare for two individuals to be able to help each other directly. One could help the other, but someone else in the chain of relationships may end up helping the person who helped. This form of generalized reciprocity means that no one worries about being taken advantage of, and everyone receives help on their request. Participants are blown away by what the group is able to "solve" for one another.

Communities of Generosity

Now imagine that kind of atmosphere, but, instead of a one-off group of around ten people, it is a diverse community of people inclined to give naturally. And it meets regularly.

When you are part of such a community where people are encouraged to give, concerns rarely arise around how much you've given. Without this structure, you might be focused on whether your own genuine needs can eventually be met. If they aren't, you could begin to feel empty, used, and unappreciated, as if no one is paying attention or caring enough to support you. However, with creating a community based generalized reciprocity, it takes just one specific practice to empower action and awaken the true potency of our networks. This allows us all to ask for what we need with purpose, vulnerability, and passion.

Yes, it may look like asking for what you need is more like learning how to take than learning how to be a part of a community, but this is the specific practice we focus on because we assure you that, while there is some of the former, the latter is much stronger if asking with purpose and clarity is done well.

Why is it so important to learn how to ask for what you need? No one can read your mind. No one can look at David and hear the new composition in his head. He has to do the work and put it into music for you to understand and connect with him. Yet, so many of us go about our lives just wishing that people could or would understand us. Instead, the OC community approach encourages members to *seek to be understood and to understand others by embracing vulnerability and curiosity, then acting on what they learn while maintaining a "give first" mentality.* Admittedly, it is not easy work, but it is essential for community functioning.

This is a core function, and a surprising difference from many groups. We contend that, the more successful the community, the more they have found a way to create a permissions-based system to encourage people to ask, demonstrate, or lead with intent, and to have that reciprocated in a way that continues to build and demonstrate trust.

The Narrow or Broad Path

As we age, we begin to think of the years we have left, not those we have ahead of us. Many are impressed by the senior citizen whose behavior is closer to that of someone in their 30s than their 70s. The people who take major trips, or those who continue to work because they feel a calling. The ones who take up something new.

In reality, the curiosity sparked by such people is driven by the fact that they continue to broaden their life, rather than shrink it. That is all a choice, as is how generous we are.

Giving—specifically, the kind of giving that comes from the knowledge of its intrinsic benefit—adds breadth to our life. Taking—or only giving in direct, proportional exchange—narrows it.

The challenge is that there are always ready excuses: "I'll have more to put in the savings account," "I simply don't have the time with the kids' practice schedules," or "I don't have much to offer anyone," even though you may very well have been helped yourself. It's not that these are not legitimate, but that they are often not the real reason that people are not more generous.

We shirk our responsibilities of helping others because we believe it will sap our energy and take away desperately needed time. But here is the issue: if you ask anyone who gives voluntarily of their time and money (never just money alone), they will share how invigorating the work is. It broadens their lives. They end up getting to know the people who they help, and, in turn, those people provide them with a greater perspective into their own lives.

Helping others, especially without expectation of anything in return, is a powerful relational currency, and it is demonstrably undervalued. Yet, it is one of the most important commodities we can build, maintain, and exchange. This isn't only about introductions; it's about helping someone move, checking in on them after the loss of a pet, or bringing them lunch when you notice they forgot theirs but were too busy to leave their desk.

Since 2017, David has explored this phenomenon and the absolute lack of value most people feel is given to intentional and thoughtful generosity. Not only is it thankless in many cases, but people are often made to feel that by asking for *any* reciprocity for their generosity with their time or connections, they are perverting that generosity. So, for many, there is seemingly no value to this type of generosity and plenty of downside.

The particular interest in the undervaluing of generosity comes from David's personal experience, though he has certainly heard many others' frustration on the topic. Despite building a community based on relationship value and a start-up focused on authentic relationships, he still regularly has experiences like those described in the next section.

The Pitfalls of Ego

About thirty times a month, David receives an ask from someone, or someone reaches out because their friend said he would be able to help them. The asks are always the same: "Could David spend his time finding someone to invest in their business? To give them a job? To make an intro to a celebrity?" Without fail, the request is missing any indication of the person's purpose; the only thing clear is that the person wants or desires it. Oftentimes, the individuals making the requests will ask David to lunch and then subtly suggest he pay for them to eat with him. In many cases, someone wants to "brainstorm" for hours on strategy for what they need.

In nearly every case, the person is either naive, selfish, or simply doesn't care that David has been clear on where he draws the line in terms of his providing support, with how his business works, or with the cost of time it takes him to meet or talk to someone as a favor. There is little recognition or appreciation of the time it takes him to call in a favor and then help the person who helps him.

Our view is that this should all be relatively straightforward. If paying for lunch costs money, then it costs money—there is no free lunch. Similarly, if you are giving time and providing skills and services that you would usually be paid for, then giving that time for a "strategic brainstorming" costs time and money too. Which is not to say that it should be repaid, as such, but that recognition of those costs is critical.

The issue is one of ego. Someone feels that what they have to offer is better and more important than that of the person from whom they are asking for help. There is, of course, irony here—they are the ones asking for help—but that doesn't make it less relevant or true. Those who are generous give their time because they want to help, only to too often be taken advantage of repeatedly by people who are not at all generous with *their* own time. Chances are, if you're reading this, you've probably experienced something similar.

But, when a community is structured around generosity and welcoming givers, individual action can be valued. Doing so adds to the ethos of the whole. Within the OC community, this is what "honoring the chain" means (see Chapter 10): it provides a data point that allows for people to celebrate everyone who was part of supporting another. It makes what is otherwise hard to visualize tangible, visible, and actionable in response.

Bad Apples, Bad Seeds

In 2017, OC community member Erik Heels joined a networking group (not Orchestrated Connecting). The group, clearly intended for "givers," was based in Boston and had started strong but burned out in less than a year. After the group shut down, Erik was asked by the group's founder for a meeting to help determine why the group hadn't succeeded. The founder was clearly a giver, but he had seeded the group with people from his own network, not with people who were primarily givers. The desired culture was not the realized culture—it became fairly obvious why the group fell apart.

Curious as to whether he could have predicted such an outcome, Erik built a start-up and developed a proprietary algorithm that used publicly available data to help discern whether people are more likely to be givers or takers. Called the RIFKIN score, Erik tested it on the now-defunct group. He discovered that (a) the group was mostly "giver-ish," but (b) some takers had joined.

Erik stresses that it's OK to have some takers in a giver-ish group, since they tend to act more giver-like when surrounded by other givers. However, you have to keep your eye on them, which the founder of the former group did not. When the group had started to struggle, the founder appointed ten "ambassadors" to try to save it. Each ambassador was charged with reaching out to a subset of the group's members. When Erik used his "givertech" to evaluate the ambassadors, however, he discovered that nine out of ten were takers! The group—and its leadership—had become infected with takers. That was the final nail in the coffin for this networking group.

Erik says he has seen this pattern again and again in groups (networking and others) of all sizes. If you let the takers in, they will invite more takers—or turn givers into takers—and soon the group will collapse. For this reason, he no longer lets members of his Treehouse networking group nominate others for membership. Givers may be good at giving, but that does not necessarily mean that they are good at spotting other givers.

Spreading Generosity

While giving helps fulfill a sense of purpose, taking likely erodes it from your life. You may have success when taking, but it is unlikely that you will feel fulfillment or happiness. In a community, it is essential to define the "give and give," to condemn the act of "taking," and to encourage everyone to be an advocate for others, even more so than for themselves. This creates true community and keeps everyone open to continued giving. If takers are not allowed—or are dealt with swiftly when they reveal themselves—everyone involved feels more inclined to continue their generosity. Communities work because their members are both givers and, when ready, willing to make their ask, trusting that, when it is their turn to ask, they will be received as another giver in need of support.

Perhaps the best part? Generosity is contagious. Why else would people continue to help strangers even in situations where such help is not necessary nor is it immediately advantageous to the person providing the assistance?

Don't just take our word for it. In one experiment, participants took part in a public good game: they were given an initial allotment of money, put into a random group of four people, and given the option of contributing some sum of money to a collective project. Each unit of money contributed only cost the person giving it that single unit, but the unit benefitted each group member +0.4 units under the rules of the experiment. Thus, contributing cost the individual 0.6 (–1 + 0.4), but the group as a whole benefited by 0.6 (0.4 × 4 – 1). Each participant took part in multiple rounds, each with different group members, so it was possible to see how prior experience of generosity contributed to future behavior.

When a participant's group members were generous in one round, that participant was more generous in the next round, even with completely different group members. Even more impressively, because of the contagious nature of generosity, the behavior of others who were never even in the same group as a focal participant influenced that participant's likelihood of later contributing to the public good. The effects extended to three degrees of separation—"from person to person to person"—showing that the behavior cascades across people who experience generosity directly and indirectly.

So, when we say that giving adds width to your life, it goes beyond simple metaphor. When people are generous with their time, their resources, or their expertise—particularly when that generosity occurs within a well-defined and committed community—there is a multiplier effect applied to each act of giving.

It is therefore a small but important detail that community members naturally give by default. In more public contexts, people can sometimes see generosity and then not necessarily be willing to give, believing that others are going to help and that help is sufficient. But, when generosity is a group norm and group members believe both in helping others and the likelihood that they will (eventually) be the recipient of generosity, the multiplier effect can work its magic.

True generosity isn't about giving a percentage of your earnings; it's about giving everything you can and wanting more, specifically so that you can give more. Personally, we've noticed that it is often those who are the most strapped for time or cash who are often the most generous.

Something is wrong with that picture.

For many, life is not so hard that you cannot help one person out for an hour a year (or even a month). Fundamentally, generosity is about not accepting your excuses. It is about choosing to continue to enrich and expand your life, finding comfort in differences through empathy and vulnerability, and accepting the reward that comes with it. It is truly most easily accomplished by embracing selflessness.

It is too easy to fall prey to the same endless paradigm of thinking that what we have isn't enough, or what we have will never be enough. It is a mental game we play with ourselves, keeping us from the present and unable to move forward. This is why we must always do self-work in addition, and as a precursor, to connecting and convening.

Our Call to Action

As you've likely realized, these principles are in a sequence for a reason. If you've gathered a diverse group of people, prompted them with something that invites vulnerability, and triggered curiosity in anyone listening to the responses, there's an atmosphere of trust, interest, and comfort. Now—whether you're meeting someone for the first time or you're next to someone with whom you've previously only had passing encounters—is your opportunity.

Take the step of asking them if you can help them in any way. "What is your biggest pain point right now?" or "What is your passion and what can I do to help?" are great questions for getting right to the point. Figure out the best way to be generous and give them some of your time and possibly more. Maybe even a helpful introduction.

Be ready to spend a little time and effort, start by simply helping, and ask for nothing in return. You'll be amazed at what happens.

10

Principle #5: Gratitude

———

I n any budding relationship, whether members of a community, recently introduced acquaintances, or work colleagues, you have a choice. Either you connect at a high level of integrity by honoring all involved in the connection-making process, or, ultimately, you diminish your relational value.

Connecting with Integrity

We already mentioned Jamil Wyne briefly in Chapter 9 in relation to generosity, but he deserves more credit, as he is where an important story—that of this book's creation—begins.

Or does it? Actually, it begins much earlier if you continue to follow the chain of connections back in time.

Honoring *Our* Connections

Jamil is Pakistani American with a wide array of interests ranging from reducing climate change to economic advancement in the developing world. That kind of background, in addition to his having done a Fulbright fellowship in Syria and Jordan, landed him in INSEAD's MBA program in Fontainebleau, France. There, in early 2018, he happened to join Noah's Organizational Behavior class. Based on mutual interests—Jamil had previously done some academic research and was interested in the kinds of organizational and institutional questions that Noah studies and teaches—they connected outside of the classroom. Jamil had spent six and a half years living and working in the Middle East, in addition to doing work in Latin America, sub-Saharan Africa, and Asia, focusing on building the ecosystems around start-ups, technology, and venture capital. The two discussed Jamil's career and whether academic life might suit him.

Ultimately, he opted not to follow that path, instead starting his own climate tech companies, but the two remained in contact after Jamil's graduation. After hearing about Noah's Office Hours experiment (discussed in Chapter 9), Jamil decided to introduce Noah to David. See, Jamil knew David because of an introduction made by his friend Aida Murad. Aida describes herself as "a global Impact Artist whose mission is to help people feel seen, heard, and loved through art."

David met Aida back in 2018. He was a highly active member of NEXUS, Rachel Gerrol's community of next-generation philanthropists and impact investors (discussed in Chapter 3). Rachel is one of those individuals whose poise and elegance in building one of the largest next-generation communities of wealth holders to catalyze change globally and create social impact directly influenced David's view on purposeful community. It, and she, led to the creation of Orchestrated Connecting. As luck would have it, David mentioned a desire to support NEXUS by moderating a panel for them. So, David was at a NEXUS conference because Rachel asked him to run a panel on art as activism, community empowerment, and a way to change minds by building community. There, he met Aida.

But wait! There's more. This is where Josh Tanenbaum comes into the picture. Josh invited David into NEXUS, knowing that his values were aligned with that community's approach. Josh's family is deeply rooted in Jewish values, social justice, and the arts (Josh is a musician himself). He also passionately supports work with refugees and now manages an active fund focused on upward economic mobility.

David was introduced to Josh by Yael Alkalay, a talented artist and systems thinking/design executive, and Eyal Vilner, a jazz musician and swing band virtuoso... We could keep going, but five "chain links" deep is a great place to stop. In fact, it's where David's "chain of connections" concept stops, and that chain is a critical piece of the Orchestrated Connecting methodology.

The chain is also an important reminder of the power of melody: that string of notes put together into something beautiful. If we are each one note, it is only when in sync and in harmony that we can create a melody together.

Honoring the Chain of Connections

"Honor the chain of connections" is *the* motto of Orchestrated Connecting. But what does it mean? At its simplest, it means that, for meaningful introductions, you—the person being introduced to someone new—should trace back through the five relationships (or as many as you can up to this number) that made the current introduction happen. What's more, you should thank each of those five people for helping make a meaningful connection. This is not an exact number, as it can be less, and occasionally more, but has been the median in the OC community for years.

On a deeper level, honoring the chain of connections involves developing a profound sense of gratitude and acknowledgment of the social circumstances that lead to any connection. Fundamentally, if relationships are the key to just about everything, as we've discussed, then nothing occurs in a vacuum: even the most chance encounters likely have peripheral actors who enabled them to occur. In fact, viewed from this perspective, there really is no such thing as a completely "chance encounter," and the practice of "honoring the chain," as David calls it, helps people realize it.

In this chapter, we bridge generosity and gratitude. After all, sharing appreciation for or with someone requires some generosity on your behalf—and the introductions that were made on your behalf are perhaps the most fundamental demonstration of generosity when it comes to community-building. We therefore dive deeper into the "secret sauce" of orchestrating connection and building stronger communities. Using specific examples from our own experiences and our connections' experiences, we highlight how the simple act of gratitude directed at the right people can work wonders.

But, before we do that, there is of course a second side to the David–Jamil–Noah introduction that warrants mentioning.

Merci? Gracias? Thank you!

It was by no means obvious that Noah would end up as a professor of organizational behavior at a business school in France. See, Noah's wife Heidi had been working for a French company in their US office in Chicago. They had asked Heidi several times to move to the company's global headquarters in Paris, but Noah had been in the middle of his PhD program at the University of Chicago and, therefore, it was not going to be feasible to move out of the country. Plus, both Noah and Heidi had minored in Spanish in college—there was no French anywhere in there, and the country hadn't really been on either's radar, despite the fact that Heidi had started visiting a couple of times a year for work.

However, in the summer of 2013, shortly after Noah and Heidi got married, Heidi's company asked again. That set the wheels in motion. As Noah was entering what he hoped might be the last year of his doctoral studies, he was open to exploring the opportunity, and he mentioned a possible interest of looking for a faculty position in France to his PhD advisor, Matt Bothner.

Matt and Noah initially connected at UChicago because of a shared interest in studying the effects of status on organizations—in particular, colleges and universities—and they had already been working on several projects together by the time the French opportunity popped up. As luck would have it, when Noah raised an interest in France, Matt had also been working on a paper on status with Frédéric Godart, a professor at INSEAD, located about forty miles southwest of Paris in Fontainebleau.

Matt suggested that Frédéric reach out to Noah, and the two began corresponding, agreeing to meet up at that year's annual, field-wide Academy of Management conference. Noah was already planning on attending, and that is where a lot of faculty recruiting activity and events take place. In 2013, it was in Orlando, Florida. In July. Because who doesn't want to be in job market-appropriate attire when it's approaching one hundred degrees and 100 percent humidity outside?

They set up a time to meet. Unbeknownst to him, Noah had been invited to meet Frédéric at an INSEAD recruiting event. Though notably underdressed for such an event—PhD students on the job market are easily identifiable as the only ones at academic conferences in business suits—Noah was introduced by Frédéric to multiple organizational behavior faculty members.

The story of introductions, job interviews, and more introductions goes on: Noah's interview visit ended with dinner in the kitchen of his future mentor, Gianpiero (from Chapter 8), his wife (also a faculty member), and a third INSEAD professor whom Noah had met on a prior trip to France. You can see where this is going: a shared research interest landed Noah with his advisor, who set off a cascade of introductions, which led to a job offer and a faculty position at INSEAD… which led to Noah's having Jamil in his class.

Noah is grateful for the opportunities presented to him that led to his academic career, and David for the NEXUS community's continuous fostering of new relationships. And, of course, now we have this book.

Recognizing Relationship Value and the Origins of Connections

Most people "behind the scenes," making important introductions, facilitating substantive meetings, and creating opportunities for relationships to form are not recognized, compensated, or even thanked for their efforts. When they are, such gratitude is the exception, not the rule.

Recognizing the relationship value of a connector isn't simple. We have described "relationship value," beginning in Chapter 2, as the social capital that exists between two individuals. Relationship value creates trust that is maintained on both sides to support each other's growth and needs, but, oftentimes, this value isn't fully recognized because identifying how a connection happened in the first place isn't always easy to pinpoint. Often, people will recognize an important connection in the simplest terms—"Oh, I met Kiara at a party." However, in order to recognize the relationship value of a connection, you have to continue to look back. Someone had to invite you, bring you, or tell you about that party. Who was that person? Did they get any credit for the invite?

Or maybe there is a different origin story. Let's say you make an important connection at a conference. Even while standing in an otherwise anonymous circle of people at said conference, your self-introduction to Greg—standing to your right—was the result of other people's input and effort. Your old business partner suggested you attend this specific conference ("It's great for networking!"), while, for Greg, attendance was the result of an invitation from his biggest client. Even in the absence of a personalized introduction, other people were still involved in your meeting. In fact, there are very few cases where the "origin" of an introduction can't be traced. "Chance encounters" are almost never 100 percent chance.

Think about the typical beneficial introduction: you become friends with someone through an original intro, and it leads to a seemingly innocuous opportunity that, two years later, turns into a joint project, an opportunity, or another critical introduction. It's not easy to remember where, how, and why it all began. But therein lies the problem: because an introduction and the benefits it ultimately provides can be separated by months or even years, people overlook the connecting notes, and these notes are a crucial part of your symphony. Sometimes, the people you meet become players in your orchestra, or you become a player in theirs. Whatever music comes from those relationships seems obvious, but the in-between notes represent all the little steps and people that made the song you play together possible in the first place.

The Orchestrated Connecting Solution

The issue David saw, time and time again, was that connections made were not explicitly recognized, which continued the endless challenge of relationship value not being appropriately honored. He needed to create a "hack" that would result in one positive action having two simultaneous outcomes. At each Orchestrated Connecting event, David asks this question: "How do you get someone to act both selfishly and selflessly at the same time?"

It is easy for someone to be generous, and we see that as selfless. That generosity has value—in this case, a useful introduction. No matter how much time, money, or energy a generous person puts into a relationship, they hand it over willingly to someone they believe would benefit from it. The selflessness is the easy part.

The hard part is to get someone to ask selfishly and take pride in the value of what's been created for them. It's much easier to say, "Thank you" than "I deserve this."

Remember that the core tenet of Orchestrated Connecting is to be purposeful: the OC community is designed to recognize the values that the collective seeks to elevate by putting the responsibility both on the individual receiving the introduction *and* the person making it.

And this is where our inherent solution comes into play. In the act of building community through honoring a chain of introductions, you both recognize everyone in that chain for their support and belief in you, and you simultaneously get to take credit not only for the incredible people you can demonstrate you know through that chain, but also for the personal success that brought you to thank them in the first place.

Another way in which David ensures that the chain of connections is honored is to remind the *connector* of their responsibility for any relationship-making to be recognized. They must take responsibility for ensuring that everyone involved understands and appreciates the importance of the value of the introduction. Another example of the person acting both selfishly and selflessly at the same time.

Honor, Trust, and Respect

We are very intentional in using the word "honoring" in this Orchestrated Connecting principle. Putting it in these terms— *honoring* the chain of connections—helps demonstrate the importance of the connections being made and the fact that value is both granted by and owed to everyone involved. Honor is a word that has little to no middle ground. While words change and meanings vary over time, the etymology of "honor" shows little variance over the years, dating back to at least the early thirteenth century. All along, it has maintained its primary meaning of conveying or bestowing respect in some form, generally with an action.

When someone acts honorably, we value them. When they are honored, we celebrate them. By facilitating honor with relationship value (by honoring the chain of connections), you create a situation that accomplishes three things at once:

1. Everyone in the "chain" takes the time to pay attention to the social dominoes that must fall in order for one valuable relationship to be formed. By expressing gratitude for the role played by each link in the chain in creating this relationship value, they are much more likely to give you their focus. Put simply, who doesn't like to be thanked?

2. The catalyst for the chain—namely, the fourth or fifth link back—is finally valued. By genuinely honoring them, you create value for, and demonstrate the value of, the origin of a relationship. Think of how rarely this is done!

3. You, as the one expressing gratitude, show yourself to be honorable and get a chain of busy, remarkable people to not just pay attention to your success but also celebrate it with you when you say thanks.

By highlighting the value of others, you are demonstrating your own value in a way that is anything but self-promoting. And, in a world where anyone and everyone can connect so easily that a great deal gets lost in the noise, sharing gratitude is a high-leverage way of warming and maintaining your connections—both of which are of course critical for personal well-being and the power of community.

Showing both your value and your values through gratitude is key to developing an ecosystem of trust that forms the foundation of community.

This is why we use the term "honor." Whether the result of an intro is relational (building a friendship, a new bond, resulting in another introduction), transactional (receiving a commission, a fee), or action oriented (being placed on a board, speaking at a conference, etc.), the value back to the person who began that chain is often unknown and unrecognized. While there are huge gray areas in the nature of these introductions, the majority of transactions that occur as the result of relationship value exchange are unregulated, invisible, and depend on the primary element that builds relationships, or quickly destroys them: trust, or the lack thereof.

Thus, the nature of connectivity and introductions must depend on honor and respect. Respect for the individual generating new connections and connectivity, and respect for those on whom it is bestowed. This is where trust comes into play, along with a strategy for how to manage that honor through the expression of gratitude. When people are put in the spotlight with or because of gratitude, their actions are no longer in the shadows.

Relationship value goes two ways. The receiver can have a direct, tangible result, or a chain of them (more on this below), but the giver must create a structure by which the recognition of that honor is able to be received in return. That, again, is the responsibility of connectors, not just the receivers.

A final musical reference. While there are many types of "harmony" and "modalities" in music, what we in the West are most accustomed to is a traditional version with tonal music. For the sake of simplicity, that means that our ears hear the basics and know when a note, or a chord, is off. This is the same in relationships. We know when something is off, or when something was off earlier in the sequence, which then affects us.

The Dynamic Nature of Communities with Honor

In the age of knighthood, the word "honor" was reserved for those privileged to be born into honorable families. To have that honor at this time bestowed by birthright and by wealth. Therefore, to be honorable was to accept the responsibility that came with that privilege. Thus, it was very easy (for some) to be perceived as honorable even while not acting in accordance with the description, while those who behaved but who that did not fit into this segment of society were not recognized as such.

In well-designed communities, honor can only be bestowed with action. Thus, in the OC community, you are only valued for the actions you take. It is an impossibility in a community of connectors to not be known for making connections. If you promise to make a connection or follow up and do not, it reduces people's perception of your value and your honor.

One of the roles played by the organizer and moderator of a community is to enforce positive behavior. Thus David's "mantra," the Orchestrated Connecting agreement (see Chapter 2), and the rules that members agree to abide by. The agreement and other rules all seem straightforward, but it is amazing how often we each forget to abide by them when busy or distracted. The more you lean into them as a practice, though, the stronger your sense of honor and the honor bestowed upon you can be. When you are judged by actions, all you have to do is stay true to your word.

When membership goes beyond showing up physically or paying into a group, and true engagement is based on committing to active participation, acting on what you say you will do, and respecting others who do so, it creates a transparent and dynamic community.

The Power of Chains

The most visible "chain links" in the world (at least to Western eyes) are represented by Audi—the four links representing the merger of four automotive companies—or globally by the Olympics, whose links are five colors and represent the belief at the time the logo was created that there were five inhabited continents in the world.

Both chain images represent mergers—combinations of countries, ideas, and people. While we have not mastered the technology yet to fully understand the complete and dynamic mapping of our relationships, the "chain" in the context of connectivity focuses on the visual of interlocking rings because a connection cannot be extended until a bond is established between each pair of connections.

Some introductions can be fleeting, meeting a need of a particular time in place—or meeting no need at all. But to meet someone and realize they could or should engage with someone else is an incredible opportunity. For a connector, the person making the introduction is not doing so casually if they have relevant expertise and the connections to match. They are judging the relevance and quality of person, the likelihood of follow-through, how the introduction might reflect on them, and the immediate need for that intro. What they are also doing is transferring or lending the relationship value they've built with an individual to the receiver of an introduction and hoping that it is valuable and well received.

Here is another moment when the chain runs the risk of becoming frayed or broken, because the "connector" in this case, as a necessity, must ask for feedback if the introduction becomes tangible or leads to another introduction. "How did that introduction work out? Was it helpful? Was that the right person?" By doing this as a regular practice, it strengthens the chain and literally avoids creating a weak link.

While "weak links" are absolutely valuable—for example, for spreading information or searching for a new job—our view is also that many of these represent shortfalls in connectivity that could've been strengthened. Obviously, someone you barely knew you worked with creates an opportunity for an intro, but it is always a shot in the dark to see if they are willing or will represent the kind of mutually beneficial tie we are talking about here. Weak links are similarly good for going fishing and expanding your network, but if you have truly built a community with purpose, then even your most peripheral links still know your value, your goals, and your needs.

A chain increases its reach with new links but its strength can fade with time. This is why the practice of honoring the chain strengthens links while continuing to add new ones.

Perpetual Motion

The patterns that appear to be unknown or random to others are some of the most powerful opportunities that a connector can intuitively spot in order to create opportunity. It is rarely just a coincidence. There must be the right framing and the right triggers to facilitate an introduction between two otherwise not-obviously-connectable people.

So, when you honor a chain by clearly stating a success you've had and why each person in that chain was instrumental in part of it, you set something in motion much greater than a single moment: you create community.

And, more than that, you allow for the unpredictable opportunities to occur. One person in our chain, Jesse Krieger, author of *Autobiography of an Entrepreneur*, was excited that we were writing a book on this topic and so introduced us to David Hancock— our publisher at Morgan James. In truth, from writing to publishing to marketing and promotion, the success of this book is the true test of the methods we're describing here. Timely, relevant introductions made at the right time.

Mathew L. introduced David to Jesse, and Cheryl H. introduced Mathew to David the same time Sarah F. did as well, and David met Sarah through Abby through Steve Z., who David met through a prior job, while David met Cheryl though Candice C. whom he met through NEXUS. There are always overlapping chains!

The Power of Gratitude

The driving force behind "honoring the chain" is of course gratitude, making it an anchor for connectivity and community. Whether simply considered as recognition for having received something from someone else or as a more general appreciation for the things you have, gratitude is associated with all kinds of benefits. In addition to social and emotional well-being, people who are more grateful are also more likely to be more empathetic, forgiving, and willing to help others. Gratitude has even been shown to benefit the creation and maintenance of relationships: people who receive gratitude feel a stronger connection to those who share it, particularly when they feel it is given authentically. Even the giver feels closer to the other person, as well.

You can see why possessing such a virtue and instilling it deeply into a community is so beneficial—but it must be cultivated and practiced, as gratitude does not come easily. Just as you cannot play anything but the simplest melody on the piano without regular practice, you're unlikely to be well skilled in giving the kind of gratitude that makes a difference to yourself or others without doing it consistently. It is not our natural tendency to stop and be appreciative of others or for what we have.

Our advice, based on practicing this ourselves, is to reach out to ask for just a couple of minutes to express gratitude when it would be honorable to do so. Such a request, whether incoming or outgoing, is always received well. And, when that gratitude is followed with silence rather than an ask, it goes even further. In fact, nearly every time David has led with an expression of gratitude and paused, the other leans in and asks what they can do. Then he responds with, "My call was to thank you; let's connect again soon." That reconnection always happens.

Honor and the recognition of others' value can take the form of an email, text chain, or group call (though we of course recommend the in-person verbal thanks or a hand-delivered thank you note). But, in the same way that small, consistent steps in changing habits add up to big differences over time, a little bit of thoughtfulness—and a specificity to your gratitude—will go a long way.

Building Community with Gratitude

Gratitude and Pasta Sauce

On the evenings of 7:47's events, at 7:47 p.m. (hence the name), everyone gathers to take on joint responsibilities and get dinner ready by 8 p.m. Later in the evening, dinner party attendees are asked to answer a question: "If you could give credit or thanks to one person in your life whom you don't give enough credit or thanks, who would that be?" It's a simple question, but it taps into some powerful emotions, prompts vulnerability, and invites immediate connection that goes well beyond the standard introductory fare.

Though now good friends, 7:47's founder Chris Schembra and David were never formally introduced. Everyone incorrectly assumed, based on a dozen parallels, that they already knew each other well. David simply approached Chris after a panel and said, "We share several close friends. I think we need to nicely chastise them for never introducing us." A friendship was born. If you know either of them, it will come as little surprise that their relationship would have an unintended ripple effect.

You see, Chris's personal willingness to be vulnerable about his childhood, overcoming addiction, and fully embodying self-love not only invites vulnerability from others but also reveals his ever-present purpose. As Chris was building the business concept for his 7:47 Gratitude Dinners, he mentioned the concept to David, who instantly recognized Chris's clarity of purpose and, because of that clarity, immediately introduced one Chris S. to a different Chris S. The result of their exchanging ideas: one of the first clients to sign on to what is now a well-established business focused on gratitude, empathy, and vulnerability.

For Chris Schembra, his purpose begins and ends with pasta sauce. It's his own recipe—now bottled—and it was created in conjunction with his goal of bringing people together around a dinner table, and around a shared recognition of the power of gratitude. Like the Orchestrated Connecting model, his rule system is critical to his community-building. The first time you attend 7:47 dinner, you come alone; the second time, you can bring a friend. By building successful first-degree relationships with over a thousand people, it was a natural fit that his business would grow with those seeking to emulate his model.

Unsurprisingly, Chris is a man of ritual. Every day, he focuses on how to be in the present, and he dives into the past by practicing authentic gratitude. It forms the foundation of his dinners, his community, and his personal ethos. By being radically curious about others and committing to creating a safe space for all he encounters at his events, he embodies what he preaches.

Great leaders like Chris have something in common that few people embody. Their vision for the future is clear in how they gather people, the choices they make, and the community they create around themselves. Chris has remained steadfast in his approach to bringing people together and sharing gratitude, maintaining his humility even with two well-regarded books, a national business model with 7:47, and growing recognition from a TEDx talk. Not to mention his thought leadership around gratitude.

To achieve the results you need for recognition, you have to be intentional in how you interact, how you follow up, and how you honor each of the relationships in your chain individually before bringing them together collectively. You can tee others up for reciprocating that openness, vulnerability, and sharing their passions by being clear not just on your value system and gratitude, but also on how you will honor what they bestow onto you.

The "Catalyst": Why Five Links?

Recognizing that it can take time, effort, and multiple introductions to make the right connection, David discovered that the origin of a powerful connection tends to be up to five links deep, on average. If you consider the person to whom the introduction was made, that makes six links, or, more colloquially, six "degrees"—though Kevin Bacon was nowhere near David's mind when he landed on five links.

Looking at the "chains" within the OC community since its inception in 2017, it became clear that, while connections can stem back through an entire life, there are "pockets" or clusters across people's networks that tend to group together. These pockets are the result of a community, a circumstance (such as college or an old job), or specific events like moving to a new city. Because each cluster is so densely connected internally—you all were in that place at the same time—it can represent the "stopping point" for honoring the chain. Because so many connections swirl around each of these, they all become comingled.

For example, consider David's involvement in NEXUS, the global social impact organization we have mentioned elsewhere in the book. While David's friend Josh brought him in and his friend Rachel is the co-founder of the community, his involvement for over a decade means his interactions there are such that he sometimes has hundreds of mutual connections on LinkedIn with someone he's never met in this community of over 6,000 people. While David will always credit Josh for bringing him in, most of his connections stemming from his involvement in this community are now generated organically.

In our view, therefore, the originator of a connection has to be a "Catalyst," the person who makes a direct, purposeful introduction based on someone expressing their needs eloquently enough to trigger the intro. The Catalyst is the person who sets it all in motion, the connector putting together two dots with a specific context and reason. This is different from a light-touch intro because it is based on hearing someone's needs and matching them with a combination of experience, emotional quotient, and relationship quotient—their ability to understand the potential mutual value in connecting two people.

So, to understand the Catalyst, you have to understand the nature of ecosystems. By design, we each have our own unique ecosystem of relationships, the overlapping networks of relationships with one person sitting in the middle of that extensive Venn diagram.

Thus, the Catalyst is the person who achieves one or more of the following at once:

1. They deepen your relationship to someone in the same ecosystem with whom you haven't yet been able to explore sufficient depth.
2. They then connect you to someone in a different ecosystem who is not in yours.
3. Subsequently, they create the opportunity (i.e., the randomness) for you to bring someone into your ecosystem by an invitation without knowing exactly what it will bring, but intentionally engaging with you to broaden your own ecosystem (separate from them).

Again, this is all about redefining your ecosystem, your network, as a purposeful community. And, by being intentional (and honorable) in how you approach each individual, you will be creating the recipe for your next Catalyst to be found, born, manifested, or run into while waiting in line for the bathroom.

Honoring Generosity with Gratitude

David met one of his closest friends, Suneet Bhatt, through an apartment building community listing about free three-month-old girls' clothing. Knocking on Suneet's door, he was met by a friendly guy with a bag of stuff. David thanked him and, before Suneet shut the door, asked how he was doing with his daughter, who had already out-grown the clothes.

While it may have been his natural instinct, David's inquiry led to Suneet welcoming him in, introducing David to aged craft beer (yes, that is a thing—an amazing thing), and the two started a friendship they maintain to this day. Suneet is an active member in the OC community and a founding advisor to an Orchestrated Connecting start-up with David.

But that's not the point of this story.

On February 4, 2018, two monumental events happened in Suneet's life. The Eagles won the Super Bowl, and Suneet lost his father, Kiran, suddenly. Kiran was a kind, incredibly sincere, and charismatic man. The two of them together radiated warmth, passion, and brought energy and enthusiasm to every room they entered.

Kiran was a die-hard Eagles fan, and he'd been waiting his whole life for this win.

Suneet is a heavy practitioner of gratitude, regularly posting on social media about whom and what he is grate-ful for. He told David about his dad's passing soon after it happened, and David did his best to be there for Suneet during this time. And then David made a call to Jonathan Ohliger.

David began with openness, sharing the pain of his friend losing his father. Jonathan heard him and responded back with sincerity to this pain.

For context, David knew his friend Jonathan played football, and had founded a company called VEEPIO, which was backed by the Eagles. Jonathan's co-founder Najee, whom David had never met, was a linebacker on the Eagles' winning team.

David asked if there was anything Jonathan (and, therefore, Najee) could do to commemorate the Eagles' win and provide Suneet and his family with some closure. Jonathan, who had never met Suneet, shared this with Najee.

Najee responded wholeheartedly with a generous offer, because he understood the trust and the vulnerability from which this ask stemmed.

A chain of trust, and now friendship, was established from a shared purpose. Najee got his entire team to sign a poster and write a note for Suneet, recognizing his father's spirit was watching over them as they finally won. They also signed a football in memory of Suneet's father.

Three years after collecting clothes and sharing in an aged craft beer, a stranger almost completely unconnected to the two friends had done something so meaningful it was truly priceless. The friends also felt a kinship, underscored by the Super Bowl win, to the point of feeling like the winning team had a guiding spirit watching over them.

Suneet wasn't someone who appreciated the gesture and then became gracious. He had consciously led with gratitude for years, and it was visible not only in his friendship with David, but also in everything he shared publicly with and about other people. The act of generosity from Jonathan was a recognition of the kind of person Suneet is, and what he does for others.

Vulnerability—the secret sauce in building trust—and a willingness to invite it in others enabled these two fathers to develop trust and brotherhood. The gratitude returned in each direction cemented a lifetime bond between them.

Suneet honored the chain, thanking Najee, Jonathan, and then David. Lastly, Suneet continued all the way back to David's friend David Monk, who initially introduced David (Homan) to Jonathan, making it all possible. When David Monk received the call, he felt what was being bestowed onto him: honor at being part of something meaningful.

Our Call to Action

While a chain can be as long as the links that continue to intersect, it is only as strong as the weakest connection between any two of those links. Sometimes, connectivity is easy, and someone becomes an old friend overnight. Other times, it takes years, shared experiences, or challenging circumstances to reach that level. Not all connections can or should end up at that level, but committing to those connections where you can create mutual value, even if only minimally, is key to allowing those connective notes to resonate. This rule—*honoring the chain*—is the solution.

If someone making an introduction knows they will be recognized and honored, it opens up an entire door of introductions that many usually keep guarded. This is truly the power of the OC community—and purposeful community in general. We don't know others for their internal lives, we only know what we each share. In the context of community, by bestowing honor on a group, that group becomes a community of honor, integrity, and *comfort* at its start. A sense of belonging follows naturally in that case.

If you are inspired by this, purposely extend your chain out, exhibiting curiosity while being purposeful in what you need, turning weak ties into strong bridges that connect you into new circles. And always express your genuine gratitude for connections made. Ask the same of others through your own behavior. In going through this process, you will continually express your value and demonstrate your intent to honor and appreciate those involved in the process.

♭ ♭ ♭

And, since you are probably wondering, yes, David has gone all the way back to Yael and Eyal—stopping to say thank you to each chain along the way to get there—to say thank you for the introduction that ultimately led to this book. As has Noah to those involved in getting him to INSEAD and in front of Jamil.

The recognition of a chain is also the beginning a new one, spurred on by generosity.

PART III

Putting the Blueprint into Action

To combine two relevant sayings, you can't choose your family and you are the sum of the people closest to you. While both are generally true, statistics show a significant decline in the time spent with family once you turn eighteen, and few stay close to the same five people they grew up with. So, where does that leave you? Well, who you surround yourself with—what you are exposed to and how you view the world—is, in the end, a choice. Your choice.

This choice is an important one: your social connections and how you engage in community is deeply connected to your physical and mental health. Your social connections also influence your likelihood of success, regardless of industry or stage of life. That means how you show up in every social situation is essential to the evolution of your career and your life.

Business development books and courses have countless recommendations on how to improve your "game," but the approach we outline here focuses on integrating your personal and professional lives as well as being clear on your needs, your goals, and who you want in your community. Stepping into action means acting with understanding and purpose, *practically orchestrating* your network.

People often complain or share that they lack the motivation to change their lives for the better, but we all know there are relatively easy ways to start expanding our circle of contacts, whether by joining a running group, a book club, a cooking class, or a new gym class. But, until and unless you take a first step in that direction, others around you, if they also lack the motivation, aren't likely to lead the way. While it's easier to do so together, someone has to start. Why not you?

If you have clarified your purpose and brought intentionality to the way you seek the people to surround yourself with, you are well on your way in this journey. Building your community and your network is fundamentally about developing the skill set to both understand yourself and see beyond yourself at the same time; to act with knowledge of your potential to impact the greater good while recognizing others' potential to do the same; and to embrace humility, vulnerability, uncertainty, and discomfort willingly as strengths rather than weaknesses to overcome.

♭ ♭ ♭

We have now considered both the "what" (experience and structure) and the "why" (overarching principles) of the Orchestrated Connecting methodology. Though we noted early on that building a formal community is not necessarily for everyone, we believe the mindset and approach we have described up to this point are invaluable for anyone who cares deeply about their network. Formal or informal, every network is a community and every gathering an opportunity to be intentional and purposeful in how you connect with others.

To that end, we now explain how to put it all together to achieve the kind of results that change lives, organizations, and industries.

11

Maximizing the Value
of Your Community

———

We start the "how to" section of this book with advice for those who would like to create and build their own community. Implied in what we say about building community is the notion that the same approach and recommendations hold if you are simply thinking of joining an existing community. That is, the work required on your part, especially in terms of first determining your own purpose and value, is going to be quite similar. As discussed in the beginning of the book, in both cases, we're talking about *any* kind of intentional community. It need not be the next Orchestrated Connecting.

You've Decided to Build Your Community... Now What?
Below is our blueprint for forming a community, with the three most important first steps highlighted at the start. These come *after* you have clarity around your own personal "why," such as a desire to address homelessness, support veterans, or get the alumni

of your school to build new programs for youth sports—whatever your purpose is. Once you have figured out your own purpose, this first exercise is foundational.

1. Start with who you know and create a list of those around you for whom you are grateful, whether those people are family, friends, teachers, mentors, or co-workers. Simply put, these should be people who add to your day rather than take away from it. Now look at them in the context of your own purpose, to see how they might fit and be passionate about your "why."

2. Think of your core two tenets. These are the beliefs that are sacred to you. It doesn't matter if others won't like them; what matters is you frame these beliefs around your value system. For example, some in the US believe no one should own a gun; others believe it is their right to do so. But both tend to agree that we should live in a society that is safe and where our loved ones can be protected. We encourage you to get to that core reason—think about the underlying rationale for a particular value, not just how that value shows up in a particular stance or opinion. This is one valuable way to foster diversity.

3. Finally, think about what you have to offer. This means your skills, your knowledge, and your existing network connections. Remember that the people surrounding you will give—to you and to whatever group they are a part of—based on what and how *you* give. Not because of some quid pro quo expectation but because of the behavior you model. What you offer is the value you provide. In some cases, that can be hosting a dinner party or providing coaching to others. Or it can be who you know!

Armed with your answers to these three questions, you can begin to figure out the specifics of your community—or the community you wish to join.

Designing a Purposeful Community

Designing a purposeful community comes from creating intentionality around each aspect of the community so that each subgroup or function feeds the others in a positive cycle of generosity, gratitude, action, and accountability. You've already taken the steps above to identify the elements that will form the foundation of your community; now, here are the steps to start building it.

Step 1: Goal

Define your overarching goal or mission. Lay out your "*why*" as well as "why now." For example:

> "I want to support communities of young girls who want to learn about and build AI companies. By supporting them with mentorship, education, and financial literacy, and surrounding them with other women and men who are allies to bring more girls into STEM and coding, we will create a new dynamic and comfort for women in this growing field of technology."

Strategy

Make your goal *action and outcome oriented* rather than topical so that everyone can see how they fit into this larger vision. This is what you want to achieve: to solve a problem, to come together around a shared pain or solution, or to bring a group together from diverse backgrounds to contribute to a common interest.

Step 2: Who

Define the type(s) of individuals that you think would belong here. Don't describe their job or status; define the shared purpose or vision you want them to embody or that they work to embody. Who are the people that, in joining your mission, will integrate well? Think of this as a descriptive term that creates a sense of purpose with everyone involved.

For the example above, the "who" might be successful founders, executives, coaches, incubators, investors, and foundation leaders who focus on AI/technology or female empowerment. It might also include men who take an active role in elevating women to leadership positions and/or run companies that have stronger gender parity in a male-dominated space.

Now, compare this list to your core list from the first question asked at the beginning of this chapter. The overlaps are likely to be the first people you wish to invite or engage to join you.

Diversity

We feel strongly that your definition of "target" individuals should speak explicitly to diversity. As discussed in Chapter 6 on diversity, we do not mean "diversity" solely from the perspective of race or gender. It should also include a commitment to diversity of socioeconomic status, age, and other factors. More generally, you should be explicit in defining *all* types of people who should feel they belong.

Engagement and Growth

How will you invite people to join you? Is there an application or nomination process? Is there an advisory board or vetting/trial period? Will one person be responsible for welcoming all potential members? Who will keep track of membership and communication? There is no single right answer, but these are important considerations. It is often up to one person or a small handful of committed members to keep the group functioning and the ball rolling.

Helping You Achieve Your Vision

The first two steps above—defining the goal and the who—are the most important and also likely the hardest to do. To further aid in your goal setting and member defining, it may be helpful to start by defining the overall achievements you want to have three years from now:

- What cause(s) have you redefined and built purpose around?
- What are the milestones you've achieved?
- What types of people have found a shared cause?
- What example have you set that others are now emulating?

As you go through the exercise of what you hope to have achieved, it can also be helpful to think about what *didn't* happen. What type of person didn't join? Does that seem right? What kind of person may join but might not be the right fit? How will you know? That brings us to the next step.

Step 3: Rule Systems

Now is the opportunity to spend some time defining your rule system. What are the principles, cultural norms, and behaviors that people should hold sacred in your network? What is expected of them, behaviorally, and what are the non-negotiables that must be met in order to allow them to continue to belong?

Your own value system is a good place to start. For example, there are some basics used in the OC community that help everyone feel like their time and presence is respected: showing up on time, being responsive to emails, not missing meetings, and so on. But the norms and expectations should go beyond these basics, of course. These behaviors should be extended to a few guiding principles for how people should act in order to contribute to the overall mission of the community and the people in it.

Think of two primary rules for involvement/engagement. There can be more, but there should be two primary rules that in combination define the type of people in your network. Think about actions that create empathy, honor, gratitude, and engender curiosity in each engagement.

The OC community's rules are laid out in the Orchestrated Connecting agreement (see Chapter 2).

Elimination

Once you have established the basic rules, you should consider the reasons someone can be removed or have their membership paused. If the introductory process for your community is clear and the cultural norms are firmly established, this should be a very rare occurrence. However, it is helpful to have the boundaries set before you start—changing the lines dividing what is and what is not acceptable after the fact is a surefire way to get people to not uphold their end of the bargain or to disengage completely. Think about how you define this so that community members hold themselves and others accountable.

Step 4: Offerings

Think about what you and the team, staff, or volunteers you bring on board can offer the community as you grow. These are the support systems that you will have in place to help the community and its rituals run. These offerings might look like:

- thought leadership

- mentorship
- activities
- relationships/connections

Geography

Related to what you will offer, where do you plan to operate? Will this be in more than one location? Will it be in person, virtual, or a combination? It is certainly possible with today's technology to operate virtually, but, in our (admittedly old-school) opinion, based on our observations of what works, commitment to the community tends to be lower with virtual-only participation.

This is not to suggest that you must travel the world, personally running events in every city with a critical mass of members like David does, but, if you want a distributed community, you will need to determine some way to make everyone feel like they belong.

Step 5: Monetization

How will your community sustain itself? This can evolve over time and be a combination of the following:

- sponsorship
- paid membership (tiered, flat, or with a free initial engagement)
- events
- conferences/retreats
- masterminds
- forums
- programmatic activity
- volunteer run and managed

As you work through these steps, keep in mind the rituals—regular gatherings and activities that reinforce a collective "groupiness"—that are fundamental to community. While aspects of rituals and events are likely to come up as you think through where you will operate and how you will sustain the community, from a financial perspective, it is worth thinking through what your community's "standard" offering will be.

How to Step into Community Leadership (and What to Look for in Other Community Leaders)

We don't want to dictate a series of "Leadership Commandments" whereby we detail the necessary actions of a community leader. To some extent, we've done that throughout the book and in this chapter. Anyone who takes up the task of creating a community will do so in their own unique way. However, we do have a few thoughts about what we believe great leadership looks like.

Critically, though the leader will have an outsized influence on the community's goals, culture, and continuity, in the end, a community isn't about the leader. Fundamentally, true leadership, when it comes to building community with intentionality, is servant leadership. A true leader is someone who respects the whole of the community rather than celebrating their role in it.

Another term we like to use is "stewardship," which implies taking care of something while also being a part of that something, as opposed to tending to it from afar or above. In this way, the example you set is what ultimately invites all other community members to lead, behaviorally and ethically, in a way that reinforces the importance of the greater good. The leader is as much a part of the community as every other member—no more, no less.

What this means is that community, as we have defined it, is about a positive cycle of actions, rather than a strict system of belonging. Even though belonging will likely arise from the experience of those positive actions, generalized reciprocity, and a coherent set of values.

So for those of you jonesing to create a collection of people willing to do your bidding, we suggest reflecting on the fact that a community isn't about "having a tribe." It is about having a values- and purpose-driven network that aligns around shared goals and actions. As with belonging, the "tribe" aspect will come about as a consequence of the alignment.

Community Member, Implementer, Visionary, or Leader?

You can actually play all these roles, but you cannot play none of them. And, unfortunately for those of you who want to avoid being in a "community," you are already playing at least one of the roles in several communities. More than you think. They just may not be intentional.

The choice you have is when you want to play a greater role—not greater in terms of being more important, but in terms of the depth of commitment and intentionality. To do so, you have to embody the principles to truly be a member, rather than just being "around" those who are also members.

Here's an example of these roles in action:

- If you show up for a march for equal pay or gender equality, your actions make you a member of this community, even if this is the only time you show up.
- If you bring others with you, you're a more committed member. You're more likely to stick around longer, engage more deeply, and feel aligned with the community's values.
- If you help make the march happen in any way—organizing volunteers, setting up, cleaning up, or taking charge of getting the necessary supplies—you're an implementer

- If you took charge and brought everyone together, you're a leader.
- And, if you developed the concept of marching for these rights, you're a visionary.

This is not a hierarchical list making the leader and the visionary the most valued. Those who are truly servant leaders know that, without the community, there is no leadership.

The Missing "Person" in These Descriptions

What makes a community—temporary or long term—purposeful isn't whether people come together for a cause and share their voices; it's whether everyone involved feels purposeful and intentional in their involvement. In purposeful communities, each person has awakened the community leader inside because all the members have been woven together into more purposeful relationships. In the end, community is something that is created over and over again by the shared actions of the members; it is not a static thing that people can simply visit and leave without contributing to it.

The individual who makes it all possible is whom we recognize as "the connector." Connection is the most necessary component to any community, and it's often overlooked. Certainly undervalued. The connector can be someone who is any (or all) of the above roles.

And how do they achieve this? How do you learn to be the connector? We'll repeat ourselves here just to make the point.

You can learn to be the connector, which exists in each and every one of us, by creating an intentionally diverse network, interacting with others with vulnerability, approaching new and old situations with curiosity, leading with and offering generosity to others, and honoring the relationships that you have made and those that have been made for you.

Your Responsibilities

Whether or not you see yourself as a group or community leader, if you spend any time bringing people together—even over a shared meal—you create that experience. And, the more you bring people together, the more you are responsible for how you do so, who you bring, and how they act with each other.

Finally, it is instructive to have a sense of what to look for in an existing community if you're looking to join instead of build one. We suggest you aim for a group that embraces gratitude as part of their core focus and shares insight into how everyone can support each other in tangible ways. It should go without saying, then, that this is how you might want to craft your own, too.

Once you stop underestimating your relationship value and that of those around you, you can truly see how surrounding yourself with people of intention and purpose grounds you and lifts all involved.

12

Orchestrating Connection in Everyday Life

––––––––––

Meaningful connections are the cornerstone of personal growth, career success, and a more fulfilling life. But connecting with intention and purpose does not happen overnight, nor by accident. It starts with deliberate action. The encouraging news is that action can be small, approachable, and well within your control.

Taking Action

A large portion of changing your connecting habits comes from simply starting: just do *something*. There are plenty of good books about changing habits out there, and our purpose here is not to repeat what's said in them, but reading this book and just assuming you'll magically have the willpower to connect, or connect differently, is a quick path to failure. So, too, is getting inspired and promising yourself that you'll run through every exercise, activity, and process we describe throughout the book within the next week. First, you're unlikely to do it, and second, when you fall short, you're likely to just give up entirely.

Habit change is hard.

Having said that, we of course do hope you are inspired and that you do start to make some changes! What we're suggesting is that you just start with reasonable, achievable goals. The more you're able to do that, the more this becomes a habit. And the more this way of engaging with others becomes part of your habit, simply another thing you do regularly and naturally, the more powerful it will be.

The good news is that, as above, starting doesn't require engaging with anyone else (yet). It starts by figuring out what your needs are. What is your purpose? What is the thing that you are drawn to most often, whether it's a part of your job or not? Remember, it should be something bigger than or outside of yourself. Something that contributes to bettering others, the world, or both. If you already get paid for it, all the better.

How can you formulate this into an impact ask? What, specifically, are your needs, and can you separate them from your wants and desires, to know that you are asking only for the most critical things and connections? This will all help you get to your "why," the beacon you will put out into the world for the "right" people to join you.

Once you're a bit clearer on this—we're not asking for a perfectly defined and understood purpose, but you have to start somewhere—running through the first three questions we bring up in Chapter 11 is where you go next. Note that you still haven't necessarily had to interact with another human being.

Finally, in terms of self-work, define your goals. More specifically, what are your one, three, and five-year goals? What do you want to achieve? What do you want to have in your life, professionally and personally? Can you imagine a life that is different or fuller than the one you have now? What is that and how does it feel?

The purpose of setting goals is not to bind you to a specific course of action that you *must* follow in the years to come. It is to force yourself to think about where you are currently and where you want to be, and to find a path on which you will set off. You are unlikely to end up in five years exactly where that five-year goal suggests—things will almost certainly change your path along the way—but you need to start out in some direction. These plans are your compass.

See? You've already done something. You're on your way.

Basic Principles

In terms of principles for utilizing the Orchestrated Connecting blueprint approach in your personal networking, let's start with what should, by now, be obvious. There is no one "right way" to be, to network, or to build community. But there are some basic tenets to guide you. It is our belief that these principles apply regardless of your goals or situation, and we start with three general categories, each of which are focused on you, the individual:

1. Ethical interacting—you interact with honor and generosity, seeking to elevate those around you; you make good on the things you say you will do; you follow up

2. Self-mastery—you accept that you cannot control anything around you except your own actions and how you react to others

3. Positivity—you are gracious in your vulnerability, acknowledging and working to overcome any biases that may pull you back toward negativity or cynicism or to see only the potential negatives in others; you have a sense of humor about things

If you walk away from this book with only these personal principles, you will already be ahead of the overwhelming majority of people. But we think these are the foundation from which even greater things are built. The core tenets of purposeful community complement the personal principles above:

- There is clarity and purpose in why you engage in a community, and you are clear on your values and goals within it. You expect the same from others.
- You regularly seek out those who are different from you, embracing your own vulnerability to encourage others' vulnerability and build deeper understanding.
- You do not tolerate "bad actors" and those who act for their own desires and wants above those of all others.

Two further principles sit between the personal and the community focused. These aim to establish the kind of culture that creates a virtuous cycle between you and those with whom you interact, ideally improving your community, building the network that meets your core needs, and encouraging growth:

4. Be intentional with whom you interact and how you want them to interact with you.
5. With each of those individuals, lean in first to address their core needs (and know those are often hard to get people to name, which is why there is an art to connecting).

Reputation and "Referability"

If you are intentional, not transactional, and you aim to address the genuine needs of those around you when you engage with them, then, every time you follow up, you grow the one attribute in life that you cannot buy, or "win," or even be born with: your reputation. As you build a solid reputation and come to understand how that positively impacts the way in which others talk about you when you are not in the room, you will have succeeded in seeding relationships that go beyond your ability to manage them.

How Are You Talked About When You're Not in the Room?

One of David's mentors, Michael Roderick, has taken the idea of reputation and made it more specific and relevant to the kind of community- and network-building we're talking about. It's also more connected to having a clear sense of your own needs and purpose. He calls it "referability."

Michael went from being a high school English teacher to a Broadway producer in less than two years by taking a very community-oriented approach to his networking style, and by recognizing the value of being "referable." He defines it as why and how someone talks about you when you're not in the room. He now runs a successful practice based on connecting: a business that includes experiential days of connecting as well as a myriad of other thoughtful ways to lead as a connector. He is the primary inspiration behind David's need to become and call himself a connector.

Michael suggests that, "When something is referable, it carves a piece of real estate in our minds." In developing this principle, Michael came up with three factors—accessibility, influence, and memory, with the acronym "AIM"—that make someone and their story more referable:

- Accessibility—People outside your primary field or area of expertise can understand the idea, your story, or whatever it is about you that you would like remembered.

- Influence—Will someone do or share something without your asking them to? This happens when your idea, concept, or story is so powerful that people feel they have to share it—the reward for doing so is simply too great not to share it. Essentially, how do you create something so cool or interesting that people are compelled to share it? Does it resonate?

- Memory—It is one thing to spend time discovering your purpose and crafting the "why" behind your story. But it is another thing entirely to learn how to tell the story, and to do so in such a way that others can re-tell that story, too. Michael suggests that people think about the language used, the emotions evoked, the simplicity crafted, and the structure. How can you craft something so memorable that not only you can share it at a moment's notice, but others can too?

Noah has taken the idea of referability and encourages his business students and executives to consider this when it comes to themselves and their job search. Much like building community starts with a clear idea of your purpose and what you bring to the table, referability comes down to how clear *and specific* you are on what you are looking for... and what you bring to the table.

Specificity here is the key, as it is going to be easier to remember someone who is both passionate about what they want to do *and* presents a very clear idea of what they are looking for than it is someone who casts a wide but vague net. The example that Noah gives in class is about someone looking to get into a product management role for the first time. Think about which of the following people is going to be easier to help—that is, *refer*—in terms of finding a role or making an introduction.

Person A approaches you and says:

> "I'm an MBA student with a background in project management, having previously worked for a medium-sized tech company. After my MBA, I'd really like to get into product management in a large tech company because it seems like a really interesting job, and it is clearly a role that is getting more popular."

Person B approaches you and says:

> "I'm an MBA student focusing my studies on management and strategy because my background as a software engineer left me feeling like I needed more soft skills and a better big picture perspective of how businesses succeed. I'd like to find a job in product management in a start-up or scale-up tech company that's working on something to address one of the UN's Sustainability Goals, perhaps focused on clean water and education, because I feel pretty strongly about tech as an actual force for good."

You may read those and roll your eyes at what seem like absurd caricatures of two people. However, these examples are based on real experiences, and they capture just how differently people tend to approach asking for introductions or help. It is subtle but necessary to phrase properly, which Person B does better in this example. For some people, there is some laziness involved, but, for most, there is an understandable belief that casting a wider, more general net means you'll "fit" more potential opportunities. However, being too general simply means (a) you're harder to remember amid a sea of people asking and looking for help and (b) you probably haven't done much of your own work in clarifying your needs and your purpose. Why should others be willing to help you if you haven't demonstrated that you've done any work for yourself?

AIM for Growth and Engagement

The principles of accessibility, influence, and memory go beyond initial encounters. While incredibly valuable when building relationships or seeking new introductions—for yourself and for others—they also add depth to existing relationships.

"Accessibility" means being open and adaptable. Your story is going to evolve, and as it does, the narrative should be clear not only to you, but to those around you as well. Your ability to be relatable increases the likelihood that others will continue to hold you and your story in mind. That means responding to others' feedback and helping frame yourself in ways that draw others in even further.

Similarly, once you have shared your initial story or powerful idea, the nature of "influence" changes. Unless you have a dramatic shift in what you are doing and the resonance of your new take on things warrants a complete retelling of your story, your influence will grow through consistent, meaningful actions. Take opportunities to offer advice, to share resources, and to celebrate others' successes, especially those that are connected to your own big idea. This is how influence grows and brings you closer still to your connections.

If you've done your ongoing work on accessibility and influence, your ability to be memorable should flow naturally. "Memory," then, is where relationships truly flourish. Small, thoughtful acts—a note of encouragement, the revisiting of a common goal, a shared memory linking your story to the person you are sharing it with—keep connections strong, and keep you top of mind. They also remind others of why they value your relationship.

Together, these AIM principles form a powerful and virtuous cycle. Accessibility grows as you remain clear and transparent in your communication, allowing relationships to evolve naturally. Influence then deepens when your actions consistently reflect your values, inspiring others to share your story or to make introductions to you. And memorability makes those introductions flow more naturally, adding new connections to the existing ones. Mutual connections reinforce those existing relationships through shared interests and increasing levels of trust.

Engaging with Intentionality and Clarity

You've understood the basic principles. You've started by taking action—any action. You have not only done the work to be clearer about your purpose and goals, you've also honed your impact ask and you've spent time making yourself more referable. Now what?

It's time to focus on engaging with intentionality and getting it from others, as well.

The Orchestrated Connecting approach is fundamentally a model of intentionality. David asks others to articulate their needs with clarity and purpose. If they aren't ready to ask, he asks them to come back when they are because he knows he can't help them until he understands what is truly driving them and why. That is, until they have their own clarity around their needs.

People are generally floored by this kind of request. Partly because they are never asked to provide real clarity, but, more than that, because he's serious about it and intentional in his approach. He sits with people and motivates them to reframe what they need into their purposeful impact ask. And, by doing so, David builds community in every conversation simply by valuing the person in front of him and then connecting them to others with similar intent.

You can do the same in your own interactions. When someone seeks your help, ask thoughtful questions to uncover what truly drives them. By modeling this clarity, you'll not only support them more effectively but also set a standard for the kind of meaningful engagement you want in return.

After all, how can you help unless you know exactly what someone else really needs?

Our Call to Action

The journey to orchestrating meaningful connections is no different from any other important journey. Start small. Start today. Begin by asking yourself: "What is my purpose?" "Who do I want to connect with, and how can I enrich their lives?" As you move forward, remember: your network is not just a reflection of who you are but also a vital instrument in the symphony of your life.

Coda

Relationships > Time + Money

Three primary currencies run our lives: time, money, and relationships. The first two are those that people most often think of—the finite resources by which you measure success and live your life. Relationships, however, are often overlooked as belonging to the same list. Much of our book has been making the case for placing "relationships" among, possibly even as the sum of, the other two.

Unsurprisingly, the three currencies are connected to one another. If there is a deficit in one of them, it's usually tied in some way to the other two and the role or emphasis placed on them. For example, if you are facing a financial deficit relative to what you would like to have, that shortfall is likely to have some connection to how you're spending your time and who you are spending (or not spending) it with... or on.

When you gain insight into your time and empower yourself accordingly, you can create strategies that give you more freedom to focus on the people you need to meet, and the community you genuinely want around you.

Our broader point is that relationships "built at the speed of trust" can change the world. Yet, relationship value remains an incredibly undervalued currency. Despite the fact that it is a powerful indicator of collaboration possibilities and interpersonal potential, people both give it away for free and ask for it for free.

But the *demand* for real relationship value outweighs the supply, leaving many of those with powerful relationships to be taken advantage of, and therefore unwilling to give away their value for nothing in return. And people who truly understand relationship value are not engaged or valued for their ability to create more of this all-too-scarce commodity.

In the finance world, undervalued commodities are jumped on: investors dive in as quickly as possible, seeking to take advantage of whatever market inefficiency has led to the misalignment between the real and perceived value of the commodity. Yet, relationship value remains undervalued—and, consequently, a genuine opportunity—because there is not yet a widespread system that can help create action around relationships, measure the outcomes, and create new possibilities. Simply put, people don't fully appreciate all that investing thoughtfully in their relationships can actually do.

Think of the time and energy, and then money and resources, that you put into building relationships with family, friends, and colleagues. With some thoughtful, *intentional* reallocation of those scarce resources, your world and the world have the chance to slowly move from tribes into purposeful communities. A deeper understanding of relationship value will be the engine that drives the evolution.

$$\text{♪ ♪ ♪}$$

During the early years of Orchestrated Connecting, many in the OC community didn't use the term "orchestrated." What people did pay attention to, however, was the idea of "making your life a symphony." And, while most people have no clue how an actual symphony is written or the mechanics of it, those things don't really matter. Over time, the notion of "orchestrating" has caught on, because its essence is more profound than simple terminology. It is a fitting label for this approach to connecting: a symphonic blend of intention, resonance, and collaboration.

For the many who have now taken up the idea of "orchestrating," we see ourselves as the conductor, standing in front of an orchestra with our backs to the watchful eyes of the audience, but with our focus on what we can make happen with all that is in front of us. We love the idea that, while we may not have written the music, we can expand it, control it, add to it, and enrich our lives.

We know there are hours of collective rehearsal and thousands of hours of individual practice that go into performing a symphony. As we orchestrate our lives, honing our own melody and joining others, we move from isolated pursuits to shared vision, intentionally and ethically becoming part of a collective purpose.

These, then, are the goals:

- to be greater collectively than you can be as one
- to have a moral compass and an ethical lens in how you view your relationships
- to be clear on who you want around you, to empower them to ask for what they need, and to encourage yourself to ask with clarity in return
- to be of service to others
- to give and give

And to do all this by amplifying others' visions alongside your own, building relationships and community that is purposeful, powerful, and humble.

We began with a nightmare. We end with a dream.

You once again find yourself walking out on a stage. The lights are again bright and shining, and, though your hands are sweaty, you breathe easy.

The applause is deafening. Familiar faces, lit by the reflective glow of the spotlight, fill your view—family, friends, even some recognizable strangers—all here for you.

You look down and you're wearing really comfortable clothes. The piano awaits, and, as you sit, a calm washes over you. The arrival of silence doesn't scare you. It empowers you.

You have created the quiet because of the anticipation of your moment. The moment you decided to make your life a symphony and change, forever, how you view the world and how the world responds to you.

Your fingers lightly hit the keys, playing not just any tune, but something new, uniquely yours.

Moments pass, then minutes, and at some point you glance out at the darkness of the hall, feeling the power and the intention of everyone, finally here, for you.

The hall could be empty, and you would still be in this moment. You know this is a dream—it will end—but you are curious where it will take you.

You are open for what comes, and you are grateful for everyone who has come on this journey with you.

You realize it's not the performance that matters. It's the journey, shared by everyone here, together, yet each also on their own path.

Your last chord echoes, a reminder that the best moments are always ahead, shaped by those who journey beside you.

Silence.

Our Impact Ask

Our passion is sharing these ideas with you and encouraging you to adopt and practice the principles in this book more fully. Our hope is that the approach described in this book inspires you to enrich your life and community by deepening relationships with curiosity, empathy, diversity of thought, and a greater valuing of those relationships, all in the spirit of shared purpose. If done at scale, the goal is to have a genuine impact on the way our world values relationships and fosters communal bonds.

If you've found value here, share this message—bring it to your community, workplace, and relationships. The world needs connectors like you who build intentional, supportive networks.

Appendix

Archetypes of Takers and Connectors

―――――

A connector's worth is regularly undervalued, as anyone who connects others is often igniting a chain that can take two to five additional introductions and three to five years to materialize into something powerful. But, when that chain of connections sparks something meaningful, it *is* powerful. This is why the work we've laid out here helps advance the trust—and therefore the speed—by which we build relationships and community.

However, trust cannot be built with everyone. We know that the world is regrettably full of "takers" and others who make the world harder for all of us. Based on our experience, here is an unscientific list of the types of people you may have run across that fit this category.

Taker Archetypes

The Collector

Knows a ton of people and always makes promises like "I'll introduce you," but never does. They keep their cards close to their chest and don't share. They may truly care about you and be an awesome person, but they just don't ever deliver when they could help you so easily. You've surely met this one. (We learned this term from Michael Roderick, whom you met in Chapter 12.)

The Ultimate Taker

Tries to use you to meet someone more prominent than you. Some people may refer to this person as a "ladder climber," but we think it's worse. They may even say they know you better than they actually do to gain leverage in their own relationships. Most importantly, they don't give back or reciprocate and can burn your bridges along with their own.

The Honied Wasp

Knows lots of rich or influential people so they think you will take a blind intro (without an opt-in) to someone who immediately pitches you on a project. Like a swarm of wasps around honey— they don't belong as most wasp species don't make honey—these people seek to profit instantly off something they did not make… without considering you.

The (Mysterious) Lurer

Reels you in with a mysterious need and asks you for coffee or a call. They know you just well enough to know you will respectfully answer them, but, when you hear their ask, you realize that this could have been mentioned in advance, and you feel frustrated and unwilling to help them. What they told you could have taken five minutes to explain, rather than an hour. You walk away, and they don't even realize there was a pond full of fish you could've helped them with if they hadn't wasted your time by being vague and putting you on the spot unnecessarily. Sometimes, fishing lures are really colorful, but you still can't catch a fish if you don't know how to fish very well.

The (Left and Right) Swiper

Doesn't check if you know someone (very easily) on LinkedIn or Facebook, or how you know them, if you do. Then they ask a favor of you while cc'ing that person. Now you find yourself either blowing off the other person and looking unkind or clarifying what you can or cannot do for this other person when the request could have been made privately.

The Selfish Asshole

Is "so grateful" that you agreed to meet with them for an hour but then only talks about themselves. They don't ask anything about you, and you walk away knowing they know nothing of your value.

The Valuator

Makes it clear that they are busier and likely more important than you, despite a strong intro with appropriate context given. The Valuator's responses often carry an air of an "Are you good enough for me?" attitude, including asking to schedule a 20-minute intro meeting as close as possible to their geographic location.

The (Unfocused, Nebulous) Nomad

Really wants to shoot the shit but doesn't really get why you are meeting them or even the value of time. The meeting goes on and on as if they have more than the hour scheduled, and you don't know what they do, how they live, or why you're spending the time meeting them. In fairness, they do often have really good coffee.

The (Over-)Eager Beaver

Keeps checking in because they just "happen to be wherever you'll be" a little too frequently and don't get the hint you are too busy to hang out because your day is filled with purposeful meetings. They aren't bad, but they don't offer much value and tend to be clingy.

The Subscriber

Thinks you wanted to be on a private bcc distribution list—which you can't unsubscribe from without offending them—for their writing. Even worse, they also keep following up. The Subscriber asks you to do stuff they need because they somehow think meeting you (without listening to you) was enough to open all doors. This profile often goes along with one of the above.

The Needy

Doesn't leave you alone even after you've politely and then firmly told them "no." The Needy dangles carrots and keeps telling you how wonderful and amazing you are. It gets arduous after a while!

The Dick

Invites someone, usually a woman, out for a business meeting and has "other intentions." (See also Drake in Chapter 2.)

The Double-Dipper

Routinely introduces people after giving each of them the impression that the *other* person is in a position to help them.

The Double-Dipper frames both introductions as if they are doing each party a favor when neither asked for it in the first place.

The Black Hole/Connector Succubus

Makes seemingly awesome intro after awesome intro, which you continually follow up on, believing the time you're spending will build more and more value. Yet, somehow, every single person, often without exception, never follows up, doesn't do what they say, and you feel like you've just wasted days of your life for that new shiny thing that now has sucked your energy dry. This is the person who keeps feeding you those people until you have to say "stop."

The Empty Box

Is always around and visible, but you can't define anything they've actually done beyond simply being around. They are an empty vessel, always seeking to fill themselves by being around more prominent people but refusing to actually roll up their sleeves or contribute in any way. These people are those who ride on the coattails of others, taking credit for the success of those who they were around. That's the Empty Box. In our world, it's the person who showed up at one of the Orchestrated Connecting events years ago, wasn't invited back, but claims credit for helping "launch" the community or sharing insight that really made this methodology what it is.

There's a reason none of these people are in our book as examples, and, every year, more and more archetypes get added from people's experience (and the others' actions).

Try *not* to be any of these.

Connector Archetypes

Now to those positive archetypes who foster relationship trust within a community.

Just as with takers, there isn't a single type of connector. In this section, we break down the primary characteristics of connectors, knowing that no two people are the same but that certain traits do pop up regularly among the people we consider to be connectors. Note, too, that we switch from third person to second person in these descriptions. We suspect, if you're reading this, you're going to find yourself much more in these descriptions than those above. Whether you possess some combination of the traits or you define your own, understanding how you resonate with and respond to others will help you better lean in to your connector capabilities.

The Convener

You may feel internally that you never get invited to the party, but you've built your own. Restless and unable to sit still, you are generally more extroverted, amazing with facial and/or name recognition, and make everyone feel important when they join something you've created. Often, you are happy when people benefit from being around each other and dismiss the value others get from being around you. Your problem? It's nearly impossible to take all the time you want to help everyone individually, and you fail to understand that convening everyone was enough in itself.

The One People Call

You'll rarely hold your own huge birthday bash, but the endless walk-and-talks, late-night or early morning calls of encouragement, and uncanny ability to remember the hard stuff everyone forgets—the anniversary of someone's death, or how someone's kid's teething is endless—endears you deeply to others. You dismiss it as something everyone does, but the truth is almost no one does it. Often, someone says to you, "I can't believe I'm telling you this… I've told no one," but you are so comfortable guarding secrets that you don't understand most people are far more gossipy than you are. Your problem? You act as a martyr for your own issues and needs, never wanting to burden others with your problems because you know how much they are dealing with.

The Shepherd/Shepherdess

While you are watching someone else's sheep (often, the alpha leader who depends on you), you act as if your role there is less consequential than theirs. You're not only their implementer, you're also the reason the flock moves. You are often incredibly organized, and you are particularly gifted in the way you sit people at a dinner, magically put the right people together in social or professional situations, and find the person who needs to be in the conversation and bring them in. Every time you shepherd those in your community, you strengthen the "flock," remembering the reason why everyone is there in the first place. Your problem? While everyone sees you as the true leader of the community, you dismiss your role because it wasn't your idea, you didn't fund it, or you don't benefit the most from it. Your concern is so operational and empathetic that you cannot see you are the reason the flock thrives.

The Thoughtful (aka "Silent Bob" or "Silent Roberta")

It's unusual for you to speak up, preferring to observe and give everyone their voice, while waiting for the right time to have yours. But, when you synthesize information and finally speak, there is no reason for anyone to speak after you. People try, but what you have done is incredibly difficult to do: demonstrate your skills at channeling the collective energy and insight in a room and distilling the true value of why people are together. Your problem? Sometimes, you don't speak up because everyone else is so forcefully "talking to hear themselves think" that time runs out before you get the chance. While you are content with knowing the importance of your insight, you deprive the room of this more often than you should.

The Silent Giver

While they say that a random act of kindness is the truest form of generosity, and you are someone who never wants a "thank you" or a gift in exchange for your generosity, you are a network weaver at the core. People trust your opinion and marvel at how you demonstrate others' value. Often, the intro you provide, the call you take, or the action you make to help others—endorsing someone without their knowing, inviting someone to an event and making sure they know the right people, or going out of your way to assist someone when they need it—is done quietly and unassumingly. Your problem? It's not what you think, which would be to tell everyone what you've done. The real issue is that you don't lead by example even when you are the *best* example of true generosity. This means that you are often the most capable of stepping up and leading but choose not to.

The Living Monument

You have the ability to strike someone to their core with who you are. And, while you are often a leader, a public speaker, a living example of who everyone wants to be, it is the depth with which you approach life—with humility despite your success—that is your most valuable trait. Your true value is in demonstrating that you see others at their core. You say "hello" to the grocery store cashier and the TSA agent, and you see how surprised they are that someone finally said hello. You help a mother with a stroller and ask if she needs more. Basically, you're Ryan Gosling. But, while there is only one of him, there are actually many of you. Your problem? Well, if you're Ryan Gosling, probably very little. For other Living Monument types, your challenge is that, while you have built yourself into someone amazing to others, you took that on individually. That means you may not have built this capability in others through mentoring or elevating those around you. While what you can give is enough when you're there, you can't always be there.

The Creative

You have always been creative and people might know you have this side, but they don't often embrace it and listen or see what you do. You have the ability to inspire others, whether with your voice, your paintings, or your comedy routines. More than that, you inspire others because you are comfortable with yourself and willing to push boundaries of social norms where others shy away, afraid of the reactions. You inspire people because you are doing what half of us thought we would do as kids until life "got in the way." Your problem? It's really hard for you to be proud of your creativity, however you demonstrate it to others, because deep down you never feel worthy, constantly trying to create more when what you've created already is amazing.

The Builder

You've always just built things. Comfortable in isolation and excellent on a team, you weave together strategy and process, simply accomplishing the things you set out to do, knowing that what you build will be for more than just yourself. That vision, and the ability to implement it, often makes you the most underrated connector because your creations are seen as tools rather than your being seen as the tool-builder that connects. But, once others begin to understand you built something that brings people together, whether it's a technology or video game, a Zen garden, or a meal that inspires conversation, others are able to see your intentions and value. Your problem? Perfection, as you always have to build more and more, fine-tuning what you're building, rather than trusting that what you've done is enough to get started, and enough to share with others already.

The Super Connector

People always ask David what makes a Super Connector. It's not the extent of your relationships, how powerful they are, or how global they are. It's that, to varying degrees, you purposefully embody many or all the traits of the other connector archetypes. In combination, that makes you uniquely you.

Gratitude

A book about community, generosity, and gratitude is naturally going to have many people to thank. And while it probably would be appropriate to honor the chain of connections with every single person we wish to thank in these acknowledgments, that would likely double the length of the book. Suffice it to say we are deeply grateful for all the connectors and catalysts who made this book possible, and who facilitated the many introductions that led us to the people whose stories we share throughout.

We want to begin with immense appreciation for our editors, Zora Knauf and Kim Yarwood. Each has helped the book's writing, flow, and clarity tremendously. What was initially two voices, perspectives, and tones alternating throughout has come together into a cohesive statement thanks to Zora and Kim's tireless work and commitment to capturing our singular voice. Zora helped mold the early versions of the book into something unified and readable, while Kim meticulously picked through every sentence and paragraph to ensure it communicated what we wanted it to. Both were critical to this book's cohesion and completion. Thank you both.

The book benefitted immeasurably from early, friendly readers who helped us further hone our voice, figure out who we were writing for, and clean up our message. Agreeing to read early versions of any book is a big commitment, and our early readers rose to the challenge. Tremendous thanks to Keirah Burrell, David

Seth Cohen, and Rebecca Schramm for your care and comments. The book is better for your input. Maritza Salazar Campo is also deserving of sincere thanks for her feedback and help on the chapter on diversity, particularly on short notice.

A special thanks to Jason Simon, who jumped on the difficult task of dealing with our cover design ideas and notes without hesitation. We have no idea how many iterations is normal for a book cover design process, but we're pretty sure we surpassed whatever that number might be. We are thrilled with where it landed, so thank you!

To the team at Morgan James Publishing—David Hancock, Krissy Nelson, and Sofia Cresta—thank you for being so welcoming, receptive, and responsive since our first contact. We appreciate the way you have ushered this project along with care, commitment, and the kind of patience needed to work with us. Deep appreciation is also due to our team at Krupp: Heidi Krupp, Darren Lisiten, Jennifer Garbowski, Terri Kayden, and Gwen Nathan. You have helped us both polish our own stories and find the right angles for our message. It has been a pleasure working with you.

This project started as a series of interviews with OC members, as Noah sought to better understand the methods and approaches used by "super connectors." Those initial interviews revealed that David had created something special in the OC community that was worth deeper exploration. David initially reached out to people in the community to ask who would be willing to speak to Noah for the project, and, unsurprisingly, nearly all of them replied quickly and positively. We extend our sincerest thanks to Ko Kuwabara, who conducted several of the interviews, and of course to all the interviewees: Kishan Alexander, Seema Alexander, Ramphis Castro, Christine Chang, Patrick Chung, Jonathan "Yoni" Frenkel, Therese Gedda, Rachel Gerrol, Mark Gordon, Lev

Mass, Shira Mazor, Wes Mendenhall, Bahiyah Robinson, Michael Roderick, Norm Rosenthal, Jenny Santi, Roxanne Sharif, Cam Snaith, and Erica Young. A note of gratitude to the hundreds of other OC community members whom we spoke with informally at events and conferences, too. Your impressions, thoughts, and perspectives helped shape the book.

Given that the book is about building community, we wanted to create a community around its launch and to build some momentum for its publication. In late 2024, we started a crowdfunding campaign to do just that, and we were blown away by the response. Our deepest and sincerest thanks to everyone who contributed: Alex Abadjis, Stuart Adam, Tessa Adams, Tina Adolfsson, Elle Ballard, Ori Barnik, Heather Beatty, Todd Benson, David Berkowitz, Rainah Berlowitz, Suneet Bhatt, Marnie Black, Juliette Blake, Pauline Borg, Peter Braxton, Keirah Burrell, Kim Carter, Nicole Casanova, Noah Caust, Christine Chen, Lori Choi, Stelios Christakos, Cristian Citu, Dorie Clark, Innocent Clement, Steve Cohen, Yosef Colish, Maya Crowne, Kristina Dalio, Angela De Giacomo, Soraya Depowski, Becky Eriksson, Eric Espinosa, Robert Ethier, Alan Ezagui, Marissa Feinberg, Cheryl Fidelman, Luke Frederick, Frank Fredericks, Jonathan Frenkel, Andrea G. Barthwell, Alexander Galambos, Jon Gosier, Asher Gottesman, Brianna Greenspan, Greg Gunn, Bulent Gurcan, Lynda Hamilton, Mickra Hamilton, Jaime Hastings, Brian Hathaway, Jennifer Hill, Graham Hill, Eva Homan, Roberto Homar, Mark Hull, Erik J. Heels, Cory Janssen, Taylor Johnson, Alex Johnston, Nadav Kadar, Mamie Kanfer Stewart, Kelly Karsnitz, Abhi Karthikey Surapaneni, Samantha Katz, Randy Kaufman, Elvin Kay, Brandyn Keating, Gray Keller, Alanna Kotler, Tamara Laine, Kiana Laurin, Andrea Lee-Zucker, Yeenee Leri, Doug Lessing, Josh Levine, Jeremy Levinson, Sophy Lo, Ron Lynch, Mike Ma, Lauren Marsicano, Suzanne McKenzie,

Farhoud Meybodi, Austin Miller, Jessica Millstone, Caroline Mindus, Andre Mirkine, Ana Morales, Glen Moriarty, David Nichols, Paul O'Dea, Jonathan Ohliger, Shiraz Omar, Danielle Patterson, Mickey Penzer, Bar Pereg, Suzanne Rabicoff, Sanjeev Rao, James Redpath, Darian Rodriguez Heyman, Marie Roker-Jones, Blayne Ross, David Ross, Michael Rowland, Steve Rubin, Christopher Ryan, Chirag Sagar, Arnaud Saint-Paul, John Samuels, Killu Sanborn, Kurt Schliemann, Rebecca Schramm, Jay Schweid, David Seth Cohen, Stephanie Sharis, Yanik Silver, Fred Smith, Michael Smith, Michael Solomon, Andrew Sossin, Matthew Spain, Sara Star, Shelley Tanner, Jonathan Tower, George Tsiatis, Christian-Joseph Turcotte, Dirk van Wassenaer, Donna Volpitta, Will Weisman, Victoria Wejchert, Jordan Wexler, Teri Whitcraft, Devon White, Jeremiah White, Carmen Wilde, Parker Williams, Tara Williams, Maximilian Winter, Leslie Wolfson, Jacqui Woodley, Shari Wynne Ressler, Alex Yastrebenetsky, Steve Zehden, and Jeffrey Zucker.

David didn't know what a connector was until Michael Roderick taught him, and he didn't see the world this way until Michael put David and Marcia Nelson on a panel where a lifelong friendship of connection began. From the early beginnings of his community, which started with a call to Rachel Gerrol, and the personal push from Dan Schawbel among others, Orchestrated began as a single event and evolved into a community, and now is in its purposeful and intentional growth phase. What it will become depends on all of us. Where life gives us lemons to make our kids too-sugary lemonade, it has to be said that, without the type of parents David has with Sidney and Norma Homan, he would not be who he is today. And without the support of Rebecca, none of this would have happened in the way it has unfolded. There is a difference between what someone thinks they have done and the reality, and, truth be told, everyone who has leaned in to support Orchestrated deserves thanks now and forever in the future.

Noah first learned about the value of connecting with people other than immediate family and close friends in the classroom. Mike Murray, his ninth- and tenth-grade English teacher, understood that it didn't much matter what was being taught so long as there was genuine care and connection between teacher and student. He is, beyond being a once-in-a-lifetime teacher, a model of generosity of spirit. Noah owes him an unending amount of gratitude. Heartfelt thanks are also owed to the other teachers and mentors—Matt Bothner, Ram Shivakumar, and Gianpiero Petriglieri—who build strong communities in and out of their classrooms, providing examples that Noah continues to aspire to. The influence of all four of these professors and educators is all over this book. So, too, are the fingerprints of Noah's parents, Sandy and Donny Askin, and his sister, Ricki Askin. An interest in and understanding of meaningful connection started with them. Finally, a huge debt of gratitude is owed to Heidi Askin, who supported Noah through the weeks and months (and years) of writing, editing, handwringing, cover selecting, and the like in the development of this book. She has created and continues to nurture the microcommunity of their family of four, and she is the force driving their stronger connection to their surrounding community. She, too, is a model of generosity of spirit.

Our final thanks are to all of you, not for reading this, but for what you are going to do now to help make this a better world.

About the Authors

David Homan is the founder and CEO of Orchestrated Connecting, a global community of connectors; Orchestrated Opportunities, an impact-focused advisory firm; and SOAR CONNECT, a start-up focused on the strength of authentic relationships. He hosts a podcast called *Orchestrated Relationships* focused on  developing relationship value, is an active classical composer, and a proud father of two. From middle-class beginnings as the son of a college professor father and nonprofit-focused mother, he has built a network reaching into the most private and incredible circles globally while maintaining a code of purposeful community-building called Orchestrated Connecting.

Noah Askin is an organizational sociologist at UC Irvine's Paul Merage School of Business, where he is also the faculty director of the Leadership Development Institute. An award-winning teacher and researcher, Noah is an expert in organizational dynamics, leadership, and culture, focusing on the informal networks of communication  and connection that drive organizational life. He has been teaching undergraduates, MBA students, and executives about networks and networking for over a decade, and his students have regularly voted him as their favorite professor. Noah's work has garnered him recognition on the Thinkers50 Radar list and has been covered by the BBC, *The Economist*, *Rolling Stone*, NPR, *Vox*, and *Forbes*. He lives with his family in Southern California.

Notes

p. x   **"Attention is"…** Simone Weil, "Letter to Joë Bousquet on April
              13, 1942," in *Correspondance* (Éditions l'Âge d'Homme, 1982),
              18.

Introduction

p. xvii   **"The highest form"…** Charlie Munger, "2007 USC Law School
              Commencement Address," May 13, 2007, University of South-
              ern California Law School, Los Angeles, CA, transcript and
              audio posted by James Clear, November 18, 2020, https://james-
              clear.com/great-speeches/2007-usc-law-school-commencement-
              address-by-charlie-munger.

p. xx   **a more common and more important occurrence…** Nicholas
              Epley and Juliana Schroeder, "Mistakenly Seeking Solitude,"
              Journal of Experimental Psychology: General 143, no. 5 (2014):
              1980–99, https://doi.org/10.1037/a0037323.

p. xx   **lonelier than at any time in recent history…** Office of the
              Surgeon General, "Our Epidemic of Loneliness and Isolation:
              The U.S. Surgeon General's Advisory on the Healing Effects of
              Social Connection and Community" (Department of Health and
              Human Services, May 2023), https://www.hhs.gov/sites/default/
              files/surgeon-general-social-connection-advisory.pdf.

p. xx   **author of *Project UnLonely*…** Jeremy Nobel, *Project UnLonely:
              Healing Our Crisis of Disconnection* (Penguin Random House,
              2023).

p. xx   **how humans have survived to this day…** Yuval Noah Harari,
              Sapiens: A Brief History of Humankind (HarperCollins, 2014).

p. xx   **crisis of loneliness in the United States…** Office of the Surgeon

General, "Our Epidemic of Loneliness and Isolation: The U.S. Surgeon General's Advisory on the Healing Effects of Social Connection and Community" (Department of Health and Human Services, May 2023), https://www.hhs.gov/sites/default/files/surgeon-general-social-connection-advisory.pdf.

p. xxi   **first decades of the twenty-first century…** Robert D. Putnam, *Bowling Alone: The Collapse and Revival of American Community*, rev. ed. (Simon and Schuster, 2020).

p. xxiii   **their residencies can be measured in terms of years rather than weeks…** Michele Reverte, "Interview: Mark Flanagan Celebrates Largo at the Coronet's First Year at Its New Location," *LAist*, May 26, 2009, https://laist.com/news/entertainment/largo-at-the-coronet-anniversary.

PART I

Chapter 1

p. 5   **just by working at it?…** Gregory Stock, *The Book of Questions* (Workman Publishing, [1987] 2013), 43, 48, 284.

p. 8   **people who do not know each other at all…** Paul Ingram and Michael W. Morris, "Do People Mix at Mixers? Structure, Homophily, and the 'Life of the Party,'" *Administrative Science Quarterly* 52, no. 4 (2007): 558–85, https://doi.org/10.2189/asqu.52.4.558.

p. 9   **it may not be that simple…** Georg Simmel, *The Sociology of Georg Simmel* (Simon and Schuster, 1950).

Chapter 2

p. 11   **Orchestrated Connecting "impact ask"…** David Homan, "The Impact Ask," *Core Beliefs* (article series), *Orchestrated Connecting*, January 13, 2021, https://orchestratedconnecting.com/core-beliefs/the-impact-ask.

p. 12   **honoring the chain of connections…** David Homan, "Honoring the Chain of Connections," *Core Beliefs* (article series),

Orchestrated Connecting, December 3, 2019, https://orchestrated-connecting.com/core-beliefs/honoring-the-chain-of-connections.

p. 18   **a communal system like a kibbutz...** A kibbutz is an intentional community, typically centered around agriculture, though the economic engines of kibbutzim have expanded in recent years. The concept is Israeli in its origins, and many still exist in the country today.

p. 18   **binds the people within those boundaries...** David W. McMillan and David M. Chavis, "Sense of Community: A Definition and Theory," *Journal of Community Psychology* 14, no. 1 (1986): 6–23, https://psycnet.apa.org/doi/10.1002/1520-6629(198601)14:1%3C6::AID-JCOP2290140103%3E3.0.CO;2-I.

p. 18   **the culture of that community...** Edgar H. Schein, "On Dialogue, Culture, and Organizational Learning," *Organizational Dynamics* 22, no. 2 (1993): 40–51, https://doi.org/10.1016/0090-2616(93)90052-3.

p. 21   **deterrent against undesired behaviors...** Abraham H. Maslow, "A Theory of Human Motivation," *Psychological Review* 50, no. 4 (1943): 370–96, https://doi.org/10.1037/h0054346.

p. 21   **deterrent against undesired behaviors...** Ronald S. Burt, *Brokerage and Closure: An Introduction to Social Capital* (Oxford University Press, 2005).

p. 26   **a majority minority community as much as possible...** A lot of David's approach stems from a study of power systems. Part of the idea built into the OC community's approach is that societal power structures will rebalance toward the actual balances of gender, race, and other shared aspects of humanity.

p. 27   **dopamine release...** James K. Rilling, "The Neurobiology of Cooperation and Altruism," in *Origins of Altruism and Cooperation*, eds. Robert W. Sussman and C. Robert Cloninger (Springer Science & Business Media, 2011), 298.

p. 27   **reinforce this giving behavior...** Ignacio Sáez, Lusha Zhu, Eric Set, Andrew Kayser, and Ming Hsu, "Dopamine Modulates Egalitarian Behavior in Humans," *Current Biology* 25, no. 7 (2015): 912–19, https://doi.org/10.1016/j.cub.2015.01.071.

Chapter 3

p. 32   **the intrinsic motivation your purpose provides...** Todd B. Kashdan, Fallon R. Goodman, Patrick E. McKnight, Bradley Brown, and Ruba Rum, "Purpose in Life: A Resolution on the Definition, Conceptual Model, and Optimal Measurement," *American Psychologist* 79, no. 6 (2024): 838–53, https://doi.org/10.1037/amp0001223.

p. 32   **primary driver of job/career satisfaction...** Daniel H. Pink, *Drive: The Surprising Truth about What Motivates Us* (Penguin, 2011).

p. 32   **pretty much everywhere in the world...** Andrew T. Jebb, Mike Morrison, Louis Tay, and Ed Diener, "Subjective Well-Being around the World: Trends and Predictors across the Life Span," *Psychological Science* 31, no. 3 (2020): 293–305, https://doi.org/10.1177/0956797619898826.

p. 32   **positivity that helps provide resilience...** Patrick L. Hill, Nancy L. Sin, Nicholas A. Turiano, Anthony L. Burrow, and David M. Almeida, "Sense of Purpose Moderates the Associations between Daily Stressors and Daily Well-Being," *Annals of Behavioral Medicine* 52, no. 8 (2018): 724–29, https://doi.org/10.1093/abm/kax039.

p. 33   **"Lives of Quiet Desperation"...** Henry David Thoreau, *Walden* (Thomas Y. Crowell & Company, 1910), 8.

p. 34   **the film *Dead Poets Society*...** *Dead Poets Society*, directed by Peter Weir, written by Tom Schulman (Touchstone Pictures, 1989).

p. 35   **the Willy Lomans of the world...** Arthur Miller, *Death of a Salesman* (Penguin Classics, [1949] 2015).

p. 35   **"rage against the dying of the light"...** Dylan Thomas, "Do Not Go Gentle into That Good Night," *The Collected Poems of Dylan Thomas* (New Directions, [1939] 1957), 128.

p. 36   **often stems from challenges and a vision beyond personal needs...** However, growth and purpose can also be driven by insecurity and imposter syndrome.

p. 37   **"Having both is best"...** Ray Dalio, *Principles: Life and Work* (Simon & Schuster, 2017), 179.

Chapter 4

p. 42   ***John Lewis: Good Trouble*...** *John Lewis: Good Trouble*, directed by Dawn Porter, produced by Laura Michalchyshyn, Dawn Porter, Erika Alexander, and Ben Arnon (Magnolia Pictures and Participant Media, 2020).

p. 48   **"connector economy"...** Adam Torres, host, *Mission Matters*, podcast, episode 76, "Building a Large-Scale Purposeful Community of Impact: Adam Torres and David Homan Discuss Building Communities," March 18, 2024, https://missionmatters.com/building-a-large-scale-purposeful-community-of-impact.

p. 50   **"network," which is primarily interested in your success...** Thanks to Gianpiero Petriglieri for the differentiating aspects of networks and community.

p. 50   **we find the key to everything...** Carlo Rovelli, "The Big Idea: Why Relationships Are the Key to Existence," *Guardian*, September 5, 2022, https://www.theguardian.com/books/2022/sep/05/the-big-idea-why-relationships-are-the-key-to-existence.

p. 54   **raw intellectual horsepower and grit don't matter...** Angela Duckworth, *Grit: The Power of Passion and Perseverance* (Simon and Schuster, 2016).

p. 54   **making sure you never eat alone...** Keith Ferrazzi and Tahl Raz, *Never Eat Alone: And Other Secrets to Success, One Relationship at a Time* (Crown Publishing Group, 2005).

p. 54   **your connections and their capabilities and connections...** Alejandro Portes, "Social Capital: Its Origins and Applications in Modern Sociology," *Annual Review of Sociology* 24 (1998): 1–24, https://doi.org/10.1146/annurev.soc.24.1.1.

p. 54   **a powerful motivational and moral force...** Alvin W. Gouldner, "The Norm of Reciprocity: A Preliminary Statement," *American Sociological Review* 25, no. 2 (1960): 161–78, https://doi.org/10.2307/2092623.

p. 54   **instrumental networking, which makes people uneasy...** Ko Kuwabara, Claudius A. Hildebrand, and Xi Zou, "Lay Theories of Networking: How Laypeople's Beliefs about Networks Affect Their Attitudes Toward and Engagement in Instrumental

Networking," *Academy of Management Review* 43, no. 1 (2016): 50–64, https://doi.org/10.5465/amr.2015.0076.

p. 56   **"birds of a feather flock together"...** Robert Burton, *The Anatomy of Melancholy* (J. W. Moore, [1621] 1857).

p. 56   **similar people are drawn to one another...** J. Miller McPherson, Lynn Smith-Lovin, and James M. Cook, "Birds of a Feather: Homophily in Social Networks," *Annual Review of Sociology* 27 (2001): 415–44, https://doi.org/10.1146/annurev.soc.27.1.415.

p. 57   **sense of oneness among a group of individuals...** Emile Durkheim, *The Elementary Forms of Religious Life* (Oxford University Press, [1915] 1947).

p. 57   **drives the sense of belonging...** David W. McMillan and David M. Chavis, "Sense of Community: A Definition and Theory," *Journal of Community Psychology* 14, no. 1 (1986): 6–23, https://psycnet.apa.org/doi/10.1002/1520-6629(198601)14:1%3C6::AID-JCOP2290140103%3E3.0.CO;2-I.

PART II

Chapter 5

p. 65   **"It's something you do"...** Daniel Coyle, *The Culture Code* (Random House Business Books, 2019).

p. 65   **the context in which the group in question finds itself...** Edgar H. Schein, *Organizational Culture and Leadership*, vol. 2 (John Wiley & Sons, 2010).

p. 68   **ten very clear principles to adhere to...** "What Is Burning Man? The 10 Principles of Burning Man," Burning Man Project, accessed June 19, 2024, https://burningman.org/about/10-principles.

p. 73   **"the impulses that animate them"...** Robert Ezra Park and Ernest Watson Burgess, *Introduction to the Science of Sociology* (University of Chicago Press, 1921), 30.

p. 73   **your reputation is not something you actually own…** Nan Lin, *Social Capital: A Theory of Social Structure and Action* (Cambridge University Press, 2002).

p. 73   **your reputation is not something you actually own…** Alejandro Portes, "Social Capital: Its Origins and Applications in Modern Sociology," *Annual Review of Sociology* 24 (1998): 1–24, https://doi.org/10.1146/annurev.soc.24.1.1.

p. 73   **share their opinions about you with one another…** James S. Coleman, "Social Capital in the Creation of Human Capital," *American Journal of Sociology* 94, no. 1 (1988): S95–S120, https://doi.org/10.1086/228943.

p. 75   **to remain active contributors…** Sameer B. Srivastava, Amir Goldberg, V. Govind Manian, and Christopher Potts, "Enculturation Trajectories: Language, Cultural Adaptation, and Individual Outcomes in Organizations," *Management Science* 64, no. 3 (March 2018): 1348–64, https://doi.org/10.1287/mnsc.2016.2671.

p. 80   **building trust more quickly and effectively…** Lynne G. Zucker, "Production of Trust: Institutional Sources of Economic Structure, 1840–1920," in *Research in Organizational Behavior* 8, eds. Barry M. Staw and Larry L. Cummings (JAI Press, 1986).

p. 80   **new people…** Note that we don't say "strangers," as people get referred in and go through the OC welcoming process, so no one is a stranger.

p. 82   **"honoring the chain" rule…** David Homan, "Honoring the Chain of Connections," *Core Beliefs* (article series), *Orchestrated Connecting*, December 3, 2019, https://orchestratedconnecting.com/core-beliefs/honoring-the-chain-of-connections.

p. 83   **ultimate drivers of behavior…** Edgar H. Schein, "Organizational Culture," *American Psychologist* 45, no. 2 (1990): 109–19, https://doi.org/10.1037/0003-066X.45.2.109.

p. 83   **critical assumption(s) in your community or network should be…** See, for example, Brené Brown, "List of Values," in *Dare to Lead: Brave Work. Tough Conversations. Whole Hearts* (Random House Publishing Group, 2018), 188, https://brenebrown.com/resources/dare-to-lead-list-of-values.

Chapter 6

p. 85   **"invite them into the conversation"...** Dan Schawbel, "Adam Grant: Why You Shouldn't Hire for Cultural Fit," *Forbes*, February 2, 2016, https://www.forbes.com/sites/danschawbel/2016/02/02/adam-grant-why-you-shouldnt-hire-for-cultural-fit.

p. 85   **San Francisco before settling in New York...** Jesse Locke, "Malcolm Cecil and the History of TONTO," *Musicworks* 128, https://www.musicworks.ca/featured-article/malcolm-cecil-and-history-tonto.

p. 86   **"We just found a method that made sense"...** Jesse Locke, "Malcolm Cecil and the History of TONTO," *Musicworks* 128, https://www.musicworks.ca/featured-article/malcolm-cecil-and-history-tonto.

p. 87   **"It was Stevie Wonder"...** Martin Porter and David Goggin, "TONTO: The 50-Year Saga of the Synth Heard on Stevie Wonder Classics," *Rolling Stone*, November 13, 2018, https://www.rollingstone.com/feature/history-of-giant-stevie-wonder-synth-tonto-752161.

p. 87   **changed the soundscape of popular music...** Will Sacks, "Stevie Wonder and TONTO: The Synth Orchestra behind His Pivotal Albums," Reverb, July 2, 2018, https://reverb.com/news/stevie-wonder-and-tonto-the-synth-orchestra-and-production-duo-behind-his-pivotal-albums.

p. 87   **changed the soundscape of popular music...** The Revolver Club, "The Synthesizer Which Helped Stevie Wonder Get His Biggest Hit," *The Revolver Club* (blog), September 17, 2022, https://www.therevolverclub.com/blogs/the-revolver-club/the-synthesizer-which-helped-give-stevie-wonder-his-biggest-hit.

p. 87   ***phily* meaning liking or loving...** J. Miller McPherson and Lynn Smith-Lovin, "Homophily in Voluntary Organizations: Status Distance and the Composition of Face-to-Face Groups," *American Sociological Review* 52, no. 370 (June 1987): 370–79, https://doi.org/10.2307/2095356.

p. 88   **enhancing creativity…** Katherine W. Phillips, "How Diversity Makes Us Smarter," *Scientific American*, October 1, 2014, https://www.scientificamerican.com/article/how-diversity-makes-us-smarter.

p. 88   **access to new perspectives…** Sarah Harvey, "A Different Perspective: The Multiple Effects of Deep Level Diversity on Group Creativity," *Journal of Experimental Social Psychology* 49, no. 5 (2013): 822–32, https://doi.org/10.1016/j.jesp.2013.04.004.

p. 88   **amplifying messages…** Cedric Herring, "Does Diversity Pay?: Race, Gender, and the Business Case for Diversity," *American Sociological Review* 74, no. 2 (2009): 208–24, https://doi.org/10.1177/0003122417714422.

p. 88   **amplifying messages…** Sylvia Ann Hewlett, Melinda Marshall, and Laura Sherbin, "How Diversity Can Drive Innovation," *Harvard Business Review* 91, no. 12 (2013): 30, https://hbr.org/2013/12/how-diversity-can-drive-innovation.

p. 88   **linked to upward economic mobility…** Raj Chetty, Matthew O. Jackson, Theresa Kuchler, Johannes Stroebel, Nathaniel Hendren, Robert B. Fluegge, et al., "Social Capital I: Measurement and Associations with Economic Mobility," *Nature* 608 (2022): 108–21, https://doi.org/10.1038/s41586-022-04996-4.

p. 88   **thwart those diverse connections from ever forming…** Raj Chetty, Matthew O. Jackson, Theresa Kuchler, Johannes Stroebel, Nathaniel Hendren, Robert B. Fluegge, et al., "Social Capital II: Determinants of Economic Connectedness," *Nature* 608 (2022): 122–34, https://doi.org/10.1038/s41586-022-04997-3.

p. 89   **access to information they would not otherwise have…** Steven Johnson, *Where Good Ideas Come From: The Natural History of Innovation* (Penguin Random House, 2010).

p. 93   **comprises mainly people of African descent…** "Made in Africa," MIA, accessed June 19, 2024, https://www.madeinafrica.com.

p. 94   **"tokens" surrounded by homogeneity…** Priyanka Dwivedi and Lionel Paolella, "Tick Off the Gender Diversity Box: Examining the Cross-Level Effects of Women's Representation in Senior Management," *Academy of Management Journal* 67, no. 4 (2024): 991–1023, https://doi.org/10.5465/amj.2021.0506.

p. 94   **A "token" is still a token…** Rosabeth Moss Kanter, "Some Effects of Proportions on Group Life: Skewed Sex Ratios and Responses to Token Women," *American Journal of Sociology* 82, no. 5 (1977): 965–90, https://doi.org/10.1086/226425.

p. 95   **"he looks more like most of the rooms we walk into, not me"…** Najee Goode, personal interview with David Homan, November 21, 2024.

p. 96   **who isn't like all the other candidates you've hired before…** Lauren A. Rivera, "Hiring as Cultural Matching: The Case of Elite Professional Service Firms," *American Sociological Review* 77, no. 6 (2012): 999–1022, https://doi.org/10.1177/0003122412463213.

p. 98   **51 percent of the country is female…** United States Census Bureau, "Explore Census Data," Census Bureau Data, accessed June 19, 2024, https://data.census.gov.

p. 99   **roughly 45 percent of the *Fortune* 500…** American Immigration Council, "New Report Reveals Immigrant Roots of *Fortune* 500 Companies," press release, August 29, 2023, https://www.americanimmigrationcouncil.org/news/new-report-reveals-immigrant-roots-fortune-500-companies.

p. 99   **more than native-born innovators do…** Shai Bernstein, Rebecca Diamond, Abhisit Jiranaphawiboon, Timothy McQuade, and Beatriz Pousada, "The Contribution of High-Skilled Immigrants to Innovation in the United States," Working Paper 30797 (National Bureau of Economic Research, Cambridge, MA, December 2022), https://doi.org/10.3386/w30797.

p. 100   **those of the others closest and most similar to us…** Ronald S. Burt, "Bandwidth and Echo: Trust, Information, and Gossip in Social Networks," in *Networks and Markets: Contributions from Economics and Sociology*, eds. Alessandra Casella and James E. Rauch (Russell Sage Foundation, 2001), 30.

p. 100   **better than it was ten years ago, and beyond…** Justin McCarthy, "Is the World Better for Gay People Than It Was 10 Years Ago?," *Gallup*, June 13, 2022, https://news.gallup.com/poll/393602/world-better-gay-people-years-ago.aspx.

p. 103   **not just a symbolic diversity officer...** Steven W. Bradley, James R. Garven, Wilson W. Law, and James E. West, "The Impact of Chief Diversity Officers on Diverse Faculty Hiring," *Southern Economic Journal* 89, no. 1 (2022): 3–36, https://doi. org/10.1002/soej.12584.

Chapter 7

p. 106   **the indivisibility of heart, spirit, and mind...** "About Us," Kokoro, accessed June 19, 2024, https://www.kokorochange. com/about-us.

p. 109   **hope that it is or will be reciprocated...** Kurt T. Dirks and Bart de Jong, "Trust within the Workplace: A Review of Two Waves of Research and a Glimpse of the Third," *Annual Review of Organizational Psychology and Organizational Behavior* 9 (2022): 247–76, https://doi.org/10.1146/annurev-orgpsych-012420-083025.

p. 109   **hope that it is or will be reciprocated...** Daniel J. McAllister, "Affect- and Cognition-Based Trust as Foundations for Interpersonal Cooperation in Organizations," *Academy of Management Journal* 38, no. 1 (1995): 24–59, https://doi. org/10.5465/256727.

p. 109   **complete ignorance of that person...** Georg Simmel, *The Sociology of Georg Simmel* (Simon and Schuster, 1950).

p. 110   **hopes of that vulnerability being rewarded and/or returned...** Oliver Schilke, Martin Reimann, and Karen S. Cook, "Trust in Social Relations," *Annual Review of Sociology* 47 (2021): 239–59, https://doi.org/10.1146/annurev-soc-082120-082850.

p. 112   **enhance perceptions of trustworthiness...** Ronald S. Burt and Marc Knez, "Kinds of Third-Party Effects on Trust," *Rationality and Society* 7, no. 3 (1995): 255–92, https://doi.org/10.1177/10 43463195007003003.

p. 114   **in addition to this ego depletion...** Roy F. Baumeister and Kathleen D. Vohs, "Self-Regulation, Ego Depletion, and Motivation," *Social and Personality Psychology Compass* 1, no. 1 (2007): 115–28, https://doi.org/10.1111/j.1751-9004.2007.00001.x.

p. 115   **draw people closer to each other…** Brené Brown, *The Power of Vulnerability: Teachings on Authenticity, Connection, and Courage* (Sounds True, 2012), CD-ROM, unabridged.

p. 115   **connecting via vulnerability…** Brené Brown, *Dare to Lead: Brave Work. Tough Conversations. Whole Hearts* (Random House Publishing Group, 2018).

p. 116   **can be receptive and even helpful…** Mario L. Small, "Weak Ties and the Core Discussion Network: Why People Regularly Discuss Important Matters with Unimportant Alters," *Social Networks* 35, no. 3 (2013): 470–83, https://doi.org/10.1016/j.socnet.2013.05.004.

p. 116   **with whom to share the potentially juicy details…** "Reputation cannot arise in an open structure." In James S. Coleman, "Social Capital in the Creation of Human Capital," *American Journal of Sociology* 94, no. 1 (1988): S107, https://doi.org/10.1086/228943.

p. 116   **but don't know well…** Mark S. Granovetter, "The Strength of Weak Ties," *American Journal of Sociology* 78, no. 6 (1973): 1360–80, https://doi.org/10.1086/225469.

p. 119   **comparable (or possibly even greater) upside…** Daniel Kahneman and Amos Tversky, "Prospect Theory: An Analysis of Decision under Risk," *Econometrica* (1979): 263–91, https://doi.org/10.2307/1914185.

p. 120   **closeness between pairs of strangers in a lab setting…** Arthur Aron, Edward Melinat, Elaine N. Aron, Robert Darrin Vallone, and Renee J. Bator, "The Experimental Generation of Interpersonal Closeness: A Procedure and Some Preliminary Findings," *Personality and Social Psychology Bulletin* 23, no. 4 (1997): 363–77, https://doi.org/10.1177/0146167297234003.

p. 120   **"What would it be? Why?"…** Arthur Aron, Edward Melinat, Elaine N. Aron, Robert Darrin Vallone, and Renee J. Bator, "The Experimental Generation of Interpersonal Closeness: A Procedure and Some Preliminary Findings," *Personality and Social Psychology Bulletin* 23, no. 4 (1997): 374, https://doi.org/10.1177/0146167297234003.

p. 121   **"To Fall in Love with Anyone, Do This"…** Mandy Len Ca-
           tron, "To Fall in Love with Anyone, Do This," *New York Times*,
           January 9, 2015, 6, https://www.nytimes.com/2015/01/11/style/
           modern-love-to-fall-in-love-with-anyone-do-this.html.

p. 121   **websites around the world…** Mandy Len Catron, "To Fall
           in Love with Anyone," TEDx Talk, TEDx ChapmanU, Or-
           ange, California, August 2015, https://www.youtube.com/
           watch?v=v8Yo-PXN7UA.

p. 121   **digital subscriptions…** Dean Baquet, "50 of Our Best," *New
           York Times*, September 21, 2015, https://www.nytimes.com/
           interactive/2015/09/21/business/media/50-of-our-best-stories-
           from-nytimes.html.

p. 126   **more liked than those who ask fewer in conversation…** Karen
           Huang, Michael Yeomans, Alison Wood Brooks, Julia Minson,
           and Francesca Gino, "It Doesn't Hurt to Ask: Question-Asking
           Increases Liking," *Journal of Personality and Social Psychology* 113,
           no. 3 (2017): 430–52, https://doi.org/10.1037/pspi0000097.

Chapter 8

p. 129   **"judgment and curiosity at the same time"…** Valia Glytsis,
           Unraveling Ambition: Living and Leading from the Inside-Out
           (Valia Glytsis Leadership LLC, 2023), 45.

p. 131   **more responsive to subtleties shared by others…** Filip Lievens,
           Spencer H. Harrison, Patrick Mussel, and Jordan A. Litman,
           "Killing the Cat? A Review of Curiosity at Work," *Academy of
           Management Annals* 16, no. 1 (2022): 179–216, https://doi.
           org/10.5465/annals.2020.0203.

p. 132   **motivate us to develop further…** Celeste Kidd and Benjamin
           Y. Hayden, "The Psychology and Neuroscience of Curiosity,"
           Neuron 88, no. 3 (2015): 449–60, https://doi.org/10.1016/j.neu-
           ron.2015.09.010.

p. 134   **"beginner's mind"…** See, for example, James Clear, "This Zen
           Concept Will Help You Stop Being a Slave to Old Beliefs," Sep-
           tember 4, 2015, https://jamesclear.com/shoshin.

p. 135   *Billboard* **number-one singles written…** Chris Molanphy, "Ariana Grande's Latest Chart-Topper Turns the Controversy into Jet Fuel," *Slate*, March 22, 2024, https://slate.com/culture/2024/03/ariana-grande-billboard-eternal-sunshine-we-cant-be-friends-lyrics.html.

p. 135   **"optimal distinctiveness"…** Noah Askin and Michael Mauskapf, "What Makes Popular Culture Popular? Product Features and Optimal Differentiation in Music," *American Sociological Review* 82, no. 5 (2017): 910–44, https://doi.org/10.1177/0003122417728662.

p. 135   **"I want to be a *marketable* murderer"…** Hannibal Buress, "Stuff about Rap and Some Other Things," track 2 on *My Name is Hannibal*, Stand Up! Records, 2010, compact disc.

p. 136   **"relaxed social settings"…** Robin I. M. Dunbar, Anna Marriott, and Neil D. C. Duncan, "Human Conversational Behavior," *Human Nature* 8, no. 3 (1997), 233, https://doi.org/10.1007/BF02912493.

p. 136   **asking or giving advice…** Robin I. M. Dunbar, Anna Marriott, and Neil D. C. Duncan, "Human Conversational Behavior," *Human Nature* 8, no. 3 (1997), 240, https://doi.org/10.1007/BF02912493.

p. 136   **enforcing social norms…** Nicholas Emler, "Gossip, Reputation, and Social Adaptation," in *Good Gossip*, eds. Robert F. Goodman and Aharon Ben-Ze'ev (University Press of Kansas, 1994).

p. 137   **talking about or judging the traits of others…** Diana I. Tamir and Jason P. Mitchell, "Disclosing Information about the Self Is Intrinsically Rewarding," *Proceedings of the National Academy of Sciences of the United States of America* 109, no. 21 (2012): 8038–43, https://doi.org/10.1073/pnas.1202129109.

p. 138   **answering the questions privately…** Diana I. Tamir and Jason P. Mitchell, "Disclosing Information about the Self Is Intrinsically Rewarding," *Proceedings of the National Academy of Sciences of the United States of America* 109, no. 21 (2012): 8038–43, https://doi.org/10.1073/pnas.1202129109.

p. 139   **"different as we move forward"…** Andrew Huberman, host, *Huberman Lab*, podcast, episode 75, "Dr. Paul Conti: Therapy, Treating Trauma & Other Life Challenges," Scicomm Media

LLC, June 5, 2022, https://www.hubermanlab.com/episode/dr-paul-conti-therapy-treating-trauma-and-other-life-challenges.

p. 140   **searching for novel experiences and situations…** Todd B. Kashdan and Michael F. Steger, "Curiosity and Pathways to Well-Being and Meaning in Life: Traits, States, and Everyday Behaviors," *Motivation and Emotion* 31, no. 3 (2007): 159–73, https://doi.org/10.1007/s11031-007-9068-7.

p. 140   **trait that was connected to the teens' flourishing…** Sylvia Y. C. L. Kwok, Minmin Gu, and Kim Kwok, "Childhood Emotional Abuse and Adolescent Flourishing: A Moderated Mediation Model of Self-Compassion and Curiosity," *Child Abuse & Neglect* 129 (July 2022): 105629, https://doi.org/10.1016/j.chiabu.2022.105629.

p. 143   **"A Theory of Human Motivation"…** Abraham H. Maslow, "A Theory of Human Motivation," *Psychological Review* 50, no. 4 (1943): 370–96, https://doi.org/10.1037/h0054346.

p. 143   **the character trait of resilience…** David Homan, host, *Orchestrated Relationships*, podcast, episode 7, "Jenny Santi," produced by David Homan, Orchestrated Connecting LLC, July 20, 2020, https://orchestratedconnecting.com/podcasts/episode-seven-jenny-santi.

p. 143   ***The Giving Way to Happiness*…** Jenny Santi, *The Giving Way to Happiness: Stories and Science Behind the Life-Changing Power of Giving* (TarcherPerigee, 2016).

p. 143   **how one builds and develops resilience…** Jenny Santi, "From Trauma to Triumph," in *The Giving Way to Happiness: Stories and Science Behind the Life-Changing Power of Giving* (TarcherPerigee, 2016), 125–73.

p. 144   **psychologist Martin Seligman…** Martin E. P. Seligman and Mihaly Csikszentmihalyi, "Positive Psychology: An Introduction," *American Psychologist* 55, no. 1 (2000): 5–14, https://doi.org/10.1037/0003-066X.55.1.5.

p. 145   **may even help slow the aging process…** Matthias Ziegler, Anja Cengia, Patrick Mussel, and Denis Gerstorf, "Openness as a Buffer against Cognitive Decline: The Openness-Fluid-Crystallized-Intelligence (OFCI) Model Applied to Late Adulthood," *Psychology and Aging* 30, no. 3 (2015): 573–88, https://doi.org/10.1037/a0039493.

Chapter 9

p. 147   **"a lack of knowledge rather than a lack of will or desire"…** Lucius Seneca and James Harris, *Letters from a Stoic: Complete (Letters 1–124), Adapted for the Contemporary Reader by James Harris* (Independently Published, 2017).

p. 151   **transactional and instrumental at worst…** Ko Kuwabara, Xi Zou, Brandy Aven, Claudius Hildebrand, and Sheena Iyengar, "Lay Theories of Networking Ability: Beliefs that Inhibit Instrumental Networking," *Social Networks* 62 (2020): 1–11, https://doi.org/10.1016/j.socnet.2020.01.003.

p. 152   **people who have done favors for us…** Alvin W. Gouldner, "The Norm of Reciprocity: A Preliminary Statement," *American Sociological Review* 25, no. 2 (1960): 161–78, https://doi.org/10.2307/2092623.

p. 152   **Reciprocity Ring exercise popularized by Adam Grant…** Adam Grant, *Give and Take: Why Helping Others Drives Our Success* (Penguin, 2014), 15.

p. 152   ***All You Have to Do Is Ask…*** Wayne Baker, *All You Have to Do Is Ask: How to Master the Most Important Skill for Success* (Crown, 2020).

p. 155   **how invigorating the work is…** A meta-analysis of the research examining the link between pro-social behavior and various types of well-being concluded there is a weak to moderate but significant positive connection between the two. However, there are many moderating factors that suggest that the link between helping others and individual well-being is robust under many circumstances. See Bryant P. H, Hui, Jacky C. K. Ng, Erica Berzaghi, Lauren A. Cunningham-Amos, and Aleksandr Kogan, "Rewards of Kindness? A Meta-Analysis of the Link between Prosociality and Well-Being," *Psychological Bulletin* 146, no. 12 (2020): 1084–116.

p. 158   **givers or takers…** Erik J. Heels, "GiantPeople RIFKIN Report #0 – Introducing RIFKIN for Connectors," GiantPeople, April 1, 2022, https://www.giantpeople.com/17137.html.

p. 158   **RIFKIN score…** Serial entrepreneur Adam Rifkin said, "You don't have to be Mother Teresa or Gandhi to be a giver. You just have to find small ways to add large value to other people's lives." Quoted in Adam Grant, "Are You a Giver or a Taker?," TED Talk, January 24, 2017, https://www.youtube.com/watch?v=YyXRYgjQXX0, 5:56.

p. 159   **collective project...** James H. Fowler and Nicholas A. Christakis, "Cooperative Behavior Cascades in Human Social Networks," *Proceedings of the National Academy of Sciences of the United States of America* 107, no. 12 (2010): 5334–38, https://doi.org/10.1073/pnas.0913149107.

p. 160   **"from person to person to person"...** James H. Fowler and Nicholas A. Christakis, "Cooperative Behavior Cascades in Human Social Networks," *Proceedings of the National Academy of Sciences of the United States of America* 107, no. 12 (2010): 5337, https://doi.org/10.1073/pnas.0913149107.

p. 160   **help is sufficient...** Milena Tsvetkova and Michael W. Macy, "The Social Contagion of Generosity," *PLoS ONE* 9, no. 2 (2014): e87275, https://doi.org/10.1371/journal.pone.0087275.

p. 164   **"help people feel seen, heard, and loved through art"...** Aida Murad, accessed February 17, 2025, https://www.aidamurad.com.

Chapter 10

p. 171   **dating back to at least the early thirteenth century...** *Oxford English Dictionary*, "honour, honor," accessed June 19, 2024, https://www.oed.com/dictionary/honour_n.

p. 175   **the merger of four automotive companies...** Chris Perkins, "The Story behind Audi's Four-Ring Logo," *Road Track*, February 17, 2017, https://www.roadandtrack.com/car-culture/videos/a32673/heres-why-audis-logo-features-four-rings.

p. 175   **five inhabited continents in the world...** International Olympic Committee, "Olympic Rings – Symbol of the Olympic Movement," accessed October 28, 2024, https://olympics.com/ioc/olympic-rings.

p. 176   **for spreading information or searching for a new job...** Mark S. Granovetter, "The Strength of Weak Ties," *American Journal of Sociology* 78, no. 6 (1973): 1360–80, https://doi.org/10.1086/225469.

p. 176   ***Autobiography of an Entrepreneur...*** Jesse Krieger, *Autobiography of an Entrepreneur: Reflections on 20 Years of Travel, Adventure & Starting Businesses* (Krieger Publishing Group, 2022).

p. 177   **all kinds of benefits...** Robert A. Emmons and Anjali Mishra, "Why Gratitude Enhances Well-Being: What We Know, What We Need to Know," in *Designing Positive Psychology: Taking Stock and Moving Forward*, eds. Kennon M. Sheldon, Todd B. Kashdan, and Michael F. Steger (Oxford University Press, 2011), 248–62, https://doi.org/10.1093/acprof:oso/9780195373585.003.0016.

p. 177   **social and emotional well-being...** Alex M. Wood, Jeffrey J. Froh, and Adam W. A. Geraghty, "Gratitude and Well-Being: A Review and Theoretical Integration," *Clinical Psychology Review* 30, no. 7 (2010): 890–905, https://doi.org/10.1016/j.cpr.2010.03.005.

p. 177   **willing to help others...** Michael E. McCullough, Robert A. Emmons, and Jo-Ann Tsang, "The Grateful Disposition: A Conceptual and Empirical Topography," *Journal of Personality and Social Psychology* 82, no. 1 (2002): 112–27, https://doi.org/10.1037/0022-3514.82.1.112.

p. 177   **closer to the other person, as well...** Sara B. Algoe, Jonathan Haidt, and Shelly L. Gable, "Beyond Reciprocity: Gratitude and Relationships in Everyday Life," *Emotion* 8, no. 3 (2008): 425–29, https://doi.org/10.1037/1528-3542.8.3.425.

p. 178   **big differences over time...** James Clear, *Atomic Habits: An Easy & Proven Way to Build Good Habits & Break Bad Ones* (Penguin, 2018).

p. 178   **"who would that be?"...** This question is the one Noah asks most frequently in his class introduction exercises.

p. 179   **begins and ends with pasta sauce...** "How the Sauce Started It All," 7:47, accessed November 5, 2024, https://www.747club.org/sauce.

p. 180   **growing recognition from a TEDx talk...** Chris Schembra, "Hurricanes, Addiction, and Empathy," TEDx Talk, TEDx-HiltonHead, November 14, 2017, https://www.ted.com/talks/chris_schembra_hurricanes_addiction_and_empathy.

p. 181   **six "degrees"…** Stanley Milgram, "The Small World Problem," *Psychology Today* 2, no. 1 (1967): 60–67.

p. 181   **five links…** Smriti Sneh, "The Real History behind 'Six Degrees of Kevin Bacon' and Why the 'Footloose' Actor Hated the Idea before Embracing It for Charity," *Fandom Wire*, February 18, 2024, https://fandomwire.com/the-rcal-history-behind-six-degrees-of-kevin-bacon-and-why-the-footloose-actor-hated-the-idea-before-embracing-it-for-charity.

PART III

p. 187   **time spent with family once you turn eighteen…** "Who Americans Spend Their Time With, By Age," data from United States Bureau of Labor Statistics, Multi-Year American Time Use Survey (2009–2019) [original data], processed by Our World in Data, "Alone" [dataset], accessed November 5, 2024, https://ourworldindata.org/grapher/time-spent-with-relationships-by-age-us.

p. 187   **connected to your physical and mental health…** Daniel W. Russell, "UCLA Loneliness Scale (Version 3): Reliability, Validity, and Factor Structure," *Journal of Personality Assessment* 66, no. 1 (1996): 20–40, https://doi.org/10.1207/s15327752jpa6601_2.

p. 187   **connected to your physical and mental health…** Robert Waldinger and Marc Schulz, *The Good Life: Lessons from the World's Longest Scientific Study of Happiness* (Simon and Schuster, 2023).

p. 187   **regardless of industry or stage of life…** Albert-László Barabási, *The Formula* (Little, Brown and Company, 2018).

p. 188   **lead the way…** Nicholas A. Christakis and James H. Fowler, *Connected: The Surprising Power of Our Social Networks and How They Shape Our Lives* (Little, Brown and Company, 2009).

Chapter 12

p. 201   **good books about changing habits…** We can recommend James Clear's *Atomic Habits* (Penguin, 2018) and Charles Duhigg's *The Power of Habit* (Random House, 2012).

p. 205   **when you're not in the room…** "I'm Michael Roderick and I'll Help You Niche Up, Package, and Position Your Ideas, and Get People Talking About You When You're Not In the Room (In a Good Way)," Small Pond Enterprises, accessed June 19, 2024, https://www.smallpondenterprises.com.

p. 205   **"real estate in our minds"…** Michael Roderick, personal interview with Noah Askin, February 11, 2021.

A free ebook edition is available with the purchase of this book.

To claim your free ebook edition:

1. Visit MorganJamesBOGO.com
2. Sign your name CLEARLY in the space
3. Complete the form and submit a photo of the entire copyright page
4. You or your friend can download the ebook to your preferred device

A **FREE** ebook edition is available for you or a friend with the purchase of this print book.

CLEARLY SIGN YOUR NAME ABOVE

Instructions to claim your free ebook edition:
1. Visit MorganJamesBOGO.com
2. Sign your name CLEARLY in the space above
3. Complete the form and submit a photo of this entire page
4. You or your friend can download the ebook to your preferred device

Print & Digital Together Forever.

Snap a photo

Free ebook

Read anywhere

www.ingramcontent.com/pod-product-compliance
Lightning Source LLC
Jackson TN
JSHW022113160625
86253JS00007B/78

*9 7 8 1 6 3 6 9 8 6 8 1 4 *